Cheers

365 Cocktails and Mocktails

For all the 'spirited' people on earth

Published in 2014 by

Om Books International

Corporate & Editorial Office
A-12, Sector 64, Noida 201 301
Uttar Pradesh, India
Phone: +91 120 477 4100
Email: editorial@ombooks.com
Website: www.ombooksinternational.com

Sales Office
4379/4B, Prakash House, Ansari Road
Darya Ganj, New Delhi 110 002, India
Phone: +91 11 2326 3363, 2326 5303
Fax: +91 11 2327 8091
Email: sales@ombooks.com
Website: www.ombooks.com

Design & Layout: Shraboni Roy
Photographer: Pravin Pol
Food Stylists: Michael Swamy, Mugdha Savkar, Ganesh Shedge
Cover Photograph: Michael Swamy
Cover Photograph Location: Hakkasan Mumbai

ISBN: 978-93-80070-29-2

Printed in India by Ajanta Offset & Packagings Ltd., New Delhi

10 9 8 7 6 5 4 3 2 1

365 Cocktails and Mocktails

Sharmila Chand

Om Books International

Contents

Acknowledgements

First and foremost, I would like to express my gratitude to two wonderful people—Ajay Mago, my cool dude publisher, and Dipa Chaudhuri, the stricter one who puts things into order. While I was full of ideas, they hit the nail on the head, and made my dream come true.

I thank all the young bartenders who have given recipes, and for whom, I became a pest, constantly asking for unique, innovative drinks' recipes. Also thanks to all the girls and boys in the PR teams of all the hotels and bars (see p. 313), who patiently coordinated the recipes and made sure they reached me before my deadlines.

Thanks to ace photographer, Pravin Pol, and food stylists, Michael Swamy, Mugdha Savkar and Ganesh Shedge, who have made each drink look so alluring. How bland the book would look without their inputs.

Neeta Dutta added her editorial touch to this book, while Shraboni Roy designed the book with care and creativity. To both, I owe my thanks.

To my loving husband, Mukul, what can I say? His belief in me gives me the reason to do what I do. His high expectations keep me going.

Last but not least, I am deeply aware that I cannot do anything without the Almighty's wish. The power to believe in my passion and pursue my dreams would not be possible without my faith in my eternal FRIEND.

iifa

Be Your Own Bartender!

What does it mean when a teetotaler presents a book on hardcore drinks? It means inexplicable passion for the subject, and a lot of hard work. Plus a great deal of fun. Fun—that's how the idea of this book originated.

One day, I stepped into a well-known bar in Delhi. Journalists have this knack of barging in at the wrong time at the wrong place. So it was at a time when the bartender was alone, perhaps on a cleaning spree of the bar. As soon as he saw me enter his territory, he started playing with bottles. One went up in the air, followed by another, and another—the ace juggler was in full form. I went up to him. He smiled. I pulled up a chair and sat in front of him, at the bar counter. He inquired politely, 'Yes, Ma'am, what would you like to have?' I said, 'Anything interesting but no alcohol, please.' He got the cue and got on with the job calmly. It was a pleasure watching him—so confident, so naughty… Soon he placed two lovely coloured drinks in front of me. 'Ma'am, which one you will have? "Sex On The Beach" or "Love Bite"?' Interesting, I thought. Within the four walls of the concrete set-up, it was tough to imagine "Sex on the Beach," so I settled for the more practical "Love Bite."

Needless to say, the drink was refreshing. That's when I decided to meet up with these artists 'behind bars' and ask them to share their simple and easy recipes to try at our own personal bars.

You don't have to be a professional to rustle up a nice drink. From the recipes in *Cheers, 365 Cocktails and Mocktails*, choose one to suit your mood each day…and to add that extra zing to your life. Begin an evening with "Wasabi Marry in The Pool!" Out of the pool, make "Tequila Sunrise"—the perfect party starter! How about a "Burning Kiss" for your lady? With a green chilli garnish? Or impress her with the pretty "Pink Macbeth" with rose petals, maybe a "Blushing Damsel." And if it's Halloween, then "Mig's Den" with glowing swizzle sticks is your best bet. Or if it's time to shake a leg and do the bhangra, then go for "Tijuana Taxi." "Here Comes the Bride" is the bachelorette-party special. Or try "Pretty Senorita" —the ultimate lady's drink. A "King Kong Bomb" at lunch breaks would help to get all that extra work done later.

Die-hard locals will be up in arms if I didn't mention "Lazeez Masala Chai." With rum and chaat masala, it is meant to give you a kick.

My favourite is "Fizzi Gal" with Irish Cream. Try it and pop by to say 'Hi' to me at fizzigal.blogspot.com.

So go ahead and be your own bartender. Cheers!

Sharmila Chand

A Glass Isn't Just a Glass

A Glass Isn't Just a Glass

Waterford crystal, cut glassware, stemware—the fancy glasses in which we enjoy a drink have not always been so fine. Like wine, liquor and liqueurs, the containers in which these beverages have been served through the ages have an interesting history.

The first record of glassware or glass shapes, as we know them today, is the clay goblet made in Iberia (Spain). This design of a small thick round bowl atop a small thick stem and round flat base, was later adopted by the Britons, as is evident from old paintings and sketches in museums. When man developed carving skills, clay goblets were followed by timber tankards, used for drinking wine till the late 10th century. During the Bronze Age, the Phoenicians taught the Britons to make a copper alloy, leading to the creation of bronze tankards.

The early Romans drank wine from goblets made of silver and clay. Art was a way of life for them and found its way into everything, including wine goblets on which were embossed intricate scroll designs of leaves in pairs, with buds.

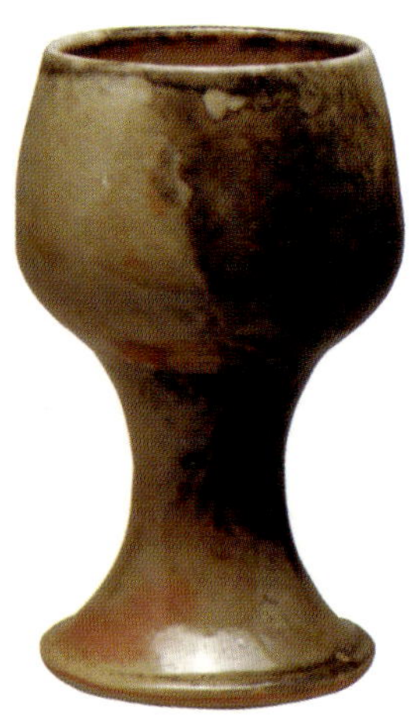

Clay Goblet

Timber Tankard

Bronze Tankard

These goblets still resembled the clay goblets in design. The turn of the 5th century AD not only brought established class distinctions in society but also differences in the quality of glassware used by different classes. A shallow silver cup with a fine stem was used by the upper classes, like rulers, priests and artists while the working class, comprising labourers, carpenters and the like, used sturdy clay goblets.

Silver Goblet

When the Saxons invaded Europe, they brought with them fine glassware and drinking horns—hollow horns of bovid animals, treated to make them safe to hold and consume liquor from. The design and quality ranged from simple hollowed horns of 'common' animals to 'rare' animal horns encrusted with gold and jewels. Perhaps the longest-surviving design in glassware in older times, drinking horns achieved the distinction of going beyond a glass to being used as property titles. Horns remained significant through the 8th and 9th century AD till the Christian church banned their use at communions.

Drinking Horn

However, in the later ages, the shape and design were recreated in several materials like gold, silver, ivory and even fine glass. It was not until the late 11th century that wine tumblers were commonly seen in England.

However, though goblets, tankards and horns were already in use, between the 12th and 17th centuries, several other types of glasses came into use—Piggins (small leather cups), Noggins (tiny wooden mugs), Goddards (pewter vessels), Stirrup cups, literally hung on stirrups, with a lid for riders on horseback to drink from and Puzzle jugs with holes around the lip which had to be stoppered with one's fingers before being drunk from. European aristocracy even drank from silver-encrusted cocoa nuts and ostrich eggs! Clear glass made a splash around the 14th century when Venetian merchants combined the skills of glass blowers and designers to make wine glasses.

Noggin

In the 17th century, the Jacobite glass was introduced by the Freemasons. Every Freemason lodge had its own style and design of glassware. The finest crystalware also appeared in the late 17th century and it is this glass that we all know so well and drink from. Since then, constant technological and creative advancement has brought about a revolution of sorts in glassware and crystalware. Tremendous research has also gone into understanding the effects of different materials on the aroma and flavour of beverages, resulting in the creation of glasses which bring out the optimal qualities of the drinks served in them.

Wine glasses and their design are based entirely on the art and science of wine making. Theories and beliefs abound on wine glasses, such as the shape and size of the glass alters the taste of the wine or using fused or cut glass impairs it (fused or cut glass does not impair the flavours of a wine). The shape of the glass though has been altered for every type of wine to be served in it, for both aesthetic and scientific reasons. This is why the choice of wine glass is important. Also known as 'Stemware', the size, shape and personal taste affects the perception of the wine being drunk. The glass highlights the visual aspect, the reflection of light, the swirl of the wine, and the aromas captured within the glass. Stemware has three parts—the foot, the stem and the bowl. The long stem facilitates holding the glass without warming the wine with the palm of one's hand, as temperature does alter the taste of wine. Another reason for not holding a wine glass by the bowl is to prevent leaving fingerprints which may distort the visual appearance of the wine while examining it for colour and clarity.

Red wines have a robust bouquet and require larger glasses with long stems and broad bowls. There are two categories of red wine glasses, characterised by their rounder, wider bowls which allow the wine to breathe. The Bordeaux glass is taller with a broad bowl best suited for full-bodied reds like Cabernet and Merlots. The lip of this glass is so designed that the wine

White Wine Glass

Red Wine Glass

on being sipped is directed to the base of one's mouth. The Burgundy glass, on the other hand, has a smaller stem but a bigger bowl and is used for more delicate reds such as Pinot Noir. The lip of the glass is designed to route the wine directly to the tip of the tongue.

A brandy glass has the same design for the bowls but with very tiny stems. Brandy requires to be warm and brandy glasses or Snifters or Brandy Balloons are designed to enable the aromas to rise to the lip, by the warmth of the hand resting under the bowl of the glass, and be captured within the tapered mouth of the glass.

White wine glasses are not only narrower with smaller bowls but also have straight or tulip-shaped sides. White wine is always served chilled and there are two factors that play a key role in keeping the chilled wine cold: the design since the straight or tulip-shaped sides reduce the surface area, thereby exposing the wine to very little air, thus keeping it cooler longer; the small bowl since it causes less contact of one's hand with the base, thus avoiding any transfer of body heat. A very popular white wine glass is the Hock glass designed for traditional German still white wines. The glass has a small coloured bowl with a clear or twisted stem and is often sold in sets of different-coloured bowls.

Brandy Balloon

Hock Glass

Champagne glasses also come in two forms—the saucer and the flute or tulip. The saucer is a glass with a broad flat bowl atop a stem and a broad foot. The flute or tulip is tall and slender with a tiny bowl and a narrow top. Designed to showcase the beauty of the sparkling wine right through its consumption, the flute retains the carbonation in the champagne till the last drop, due to the small surface area of the lip of the glass. It also shows off the tiny streams of bubbles and hence is more conducive to use than the saucers. A barman's favourite, it certainly takes up lesser cabinet space than the saucer!

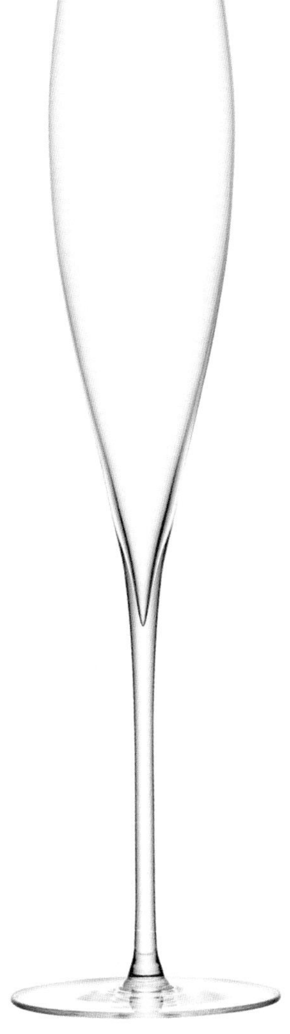

Champagne Glass

Then there is the all-purpose wine glass used by most restaurants as using assorted glassware is expensive. The all-purpose glass is all right when it comes to tasting wines or drinking table wines or at a soirée, but definitely not for a multi-course wine pairing dinner.

Sherry glassware is small and designed for serving aromatic drinks like sherry, port, liqueurs and shooters. Usually these glasses have straight sides and hold a small quantity of liquid, making them ideal for aperitifs or quick small drinks. The ISO standard for these glasses is 120 ml.

For whiskey, there is the Roly Poly, the Old Fashioned or the Tumbler. A good

Roly Poly

Old Fashioned

Shot Glasses

whiskey or scotch on a cold wet evening is a delightful experience and hence should be consumed using the right glass. Good malt must be drunk from a glass that tapers very slightly at the mouth, trapping the aromas and sending them straight to your nose as you sip. Only one-third of the glass is filled whether the whiskey or scotch is served neat or over ice or with water. The extra empty space in the glass allows for the aromas to heighten as they come in contact with oxygen. A dash of water mellows the flavour of whiskey and scotch and ice shocks the drink hiding its most potent flavours. Ideally, whiskey is never downed in a single gulp but rolled around on the palate which helps to imbibe all the flavour, distinguished by a salty and smoky aroma which is only heightened with the age of the scotch. Try and stay away from the freebie glasses that come from brewers as these being made in bulk, lack the intricate detailing required to bring out the optimal pleasure of the drink. Spend a little in good quality glasses that make the whole experience wonderful.

When it comes to cocktails, glassware takes on a whole new dimension. Here flavours, textures and colours are mixed, blended, shaken and stirred. The flare and drama involved when using a tumbler or shaker, be it made of glass or metal, takes on a whole new meaning as a lot of the drinks have an acidic base, are often a combination of two or more liquors and almost always poured over crushed ice or ice cubes. Here the

Martini Glass

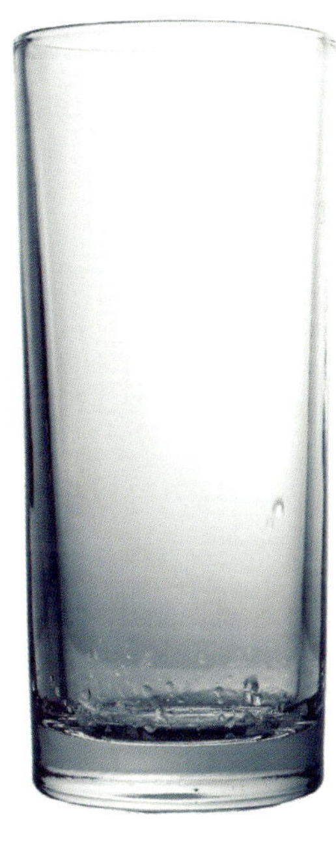

Tom Collins

Hurricane Glass

Cocktail Glass

favourite would be the Martini or other cocktail glasses which are relatively 'V' shaped. These glasses are so shaped that one can see the whole range of colours and textures of a drink. The shape also allows for a multitude of garnishes to be used.

Tall glasses like Tom Collins and Hurricane are best for drinks which require tons of ice. Rum, vodka, gin and cocktails like mojitos are best served in these glasses.

Daiquiris and Margaritas are served in glasses styled for the purpose. These glasses have a bulbous base, topped with a saucer and wide lip. The cocktail is poured over a heap of crushed ice, creating a visual treat—the drink looks pretty at the base with hints of coloured ice on top. The glass allows the drink to be sipped as the ice recedes, ensuring the drink remains chilled throughout.

Michael Swamy
Food Stylist, Photographer and Writer

Setting up a Bar

Tips for Setting Up a Home Bar

As someone who has been feeding guests since the age of eight, hospitality runs in the blood. Now with a passion for wine, food and generally having a good time, I've also developed a talent for entertaining at home.

A home bar to me isn't about its physical presence; it's about the people drinking from it. However, whether you are setting up a bar for personal use or to entertain friends, it needs a good range of quality spirits!

I'd rather supply all the drinks when I'm the one entertaining to avoid serving wine which is unsettled or unsuitable. I insist on pouring the wine which not only prevents my pet hate of guests from filling the wine to the top of the glass but also eliminates potential embarrassment when they spill wine on furniture.

Another no no, is to think of your home bar as a cheaper alternative to the wine or cocktail bar. For the same price as a bottle you'd drink in your

Ice Crusher

Shaker

Peg Measure

local hangout, you could purchase a delicious, memorable bottle of wine from independent wine merchants — you'll also

Strainer

benefit from their expertise when choosing for an occasion or food matching.

A good home bar should be both, a place to start and end an evening. So it's always good to stock a range of light and heavier drinks, including beer.

My first love is wine and I'd always recommend a good bottle of bubbly; this doesn't have to be from a big Champagne house. Smaller, lesser-known sparkling wines can be just as wonderful at a fraction of the price. Then add a couple of whites, a rosé, a few reds and a good dessert wine. Glassware is key and good quality crystal glass will really enhance your guests' enjoyment.

Always, always have a Champagne bucket with plenty of ice and water, as that is the only way to chill a bottle of wine. Sticking a bottle of good white wine in the freezer is NOT cool!

When it comes to cocktails, I'm less of an expert but Michele Notaro, a mixologist from The Gore Hotel in London, agrees that the job of a bartender is to delight your guests. Michele, who has worked at some of London's best hotels and restaurants, including The Savoy, says that any home bar worth its salt must have the six key spirits: gin, vodka, rum, tequila, whisky and brandy.

For liqueurs, you'll need sweet and dry vermouth, Angosturas bitters and an orange liqueur. Tonic water, lemonade, cola, soda, gomme syrup, cranberry, orange, apple, pineapple and tomato juice are the essential mixers. You can't have a cocktail without the theatre and for this you'll need a Boston glass, Boston shaker, a measure, muddler, knife,

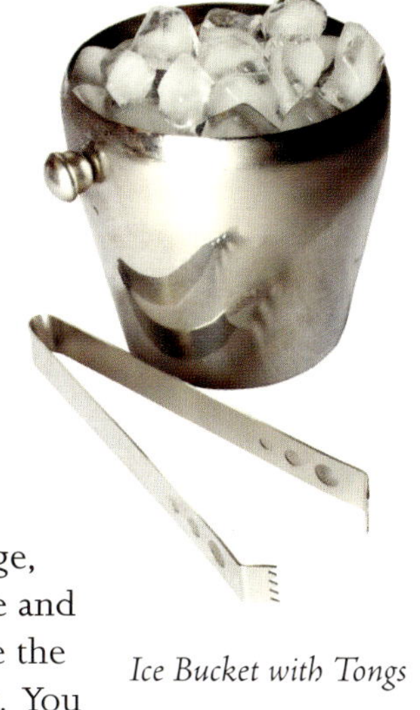

Ice Bucket with Tongs

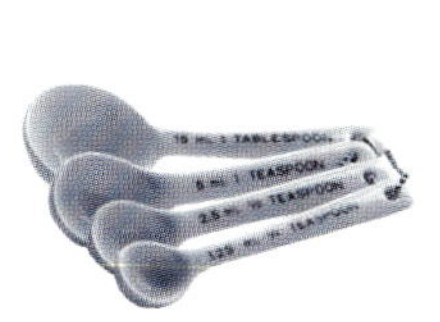

Spoon Measures

Measuring Jug

Bar Spoon
Melon Baller
Ice Cream Scoop
Juicers
Grater
Bottle Openers
Whisker
Citrus Zester
Muddler
Chopping Board and Knife

Cocktail Sticks

cocktail spoon, a strainer (and a double strainer if you're partial to Martinis). The cocktail should look stunning too, so don't forget cocktail sticks, slices of lime, lemon, orange, apple, sprigs of mint and for the Martini lover, olives.

To create a cocktail that they'll love, Michele firsts asks his guests three questions: 'Which spirits do you like?', 'Do you like sweet, bitter or sour?' and 'Do you like the alcohol to be strong or weak?' Of course, some people prefer their drink without any alcohol and Michele does a mean mocktail simply by muddling fresh berries, adding cranberry, apple juice and a touch of gomme syrup.

All the above are essential ingredients for a home bar but the most important ingredient is YOU. Research and practice making and serving drinks, ensure that you're well prepared for your guests—ice bags and Champagne bucket ready, lemons sliced and red wines decanted. Stay calm, ensure that your guests' glasses are never empty, but most of all, have a ball!

Cheers!

Chix Chandaria
Wine Lover and Home Hospitality Expert

Tricks and Techniques

Floating means adding a layer of liquor or liqueur on top of a drink.

Layering involves adding many liquors or liqueurs, one on top of the other, without mixing them. To make layered drinks, pour the heaviest (highest density) liquor or liqueur first, then slowly pour the lighter ones on top. Use the back of a bar spoon when layering.

Frosting a Glass

To frost a glass, just put it in the freezer for about an hour. For better frosting, dip the glass in water, shake off any excess water and put it in the freezer for about an hour. Always handle the glass by its stem or bottom.

Chilling a Glass

The best way to chill a glass is by putting it in the refrigerator for about 20 minutes. For lack of time, put ice in the glass and fill it with water. Let it set for a minute and drain out the ice and water.

Making Lemon Peel Curls

Take a channel knife with a sharp hole through which you can cut a small groove in the skin of the fruit, creating a long spiral length of lemon peel. Remove the small nubs at each end of the lemon.

Start cutting at one end in a line towards the other, maintaining steady downward pressure so the blade will cut into the maximum skin. When the cut is ¼- inch long, turn the knife sharply to the left and cut in a downward spiral, leaving a ½-inch strip of peel on the fruit. Cut all the way to the other pole, and end the cut as you began. You will get ½-inch-wide spiral peel which has to be cut from the lemon.

Likewise, carefully cut the second spiral peel from the lemon, keeping the knife tilted slightly inward toward the fruit to avoid cutting through the peel.

Store the peels in ice water and the spiral will tighten up and become springy.

Place the spiral garnish in the glass before the ice and ingredients. Hook the curved end of the peel over the rim of the glass and drape the remaining peel in a spiral down inside the glass until it reaches the bottom. The ice will hold the garnish in place.

Flaming

Heat the alcohol in a saucepan over medium heat. Warm it until bubbles begin to form on the edge of the saucepan. Use a long match to ignite the liquor and then pour it into a drink.

Flaming Brandy: First, heat the brandy snifter. Then pour warmed brandy into the snifter and ignite.

Tip: Liquor may be preheated in the microwave for about 12 seconds.

Caution: Be very careful. When flaming, make sure to have baking soda and a wet towel in case of an accident.

Rimming

Moisten the rim of the glass with juice, syrup or liqueur as per the taste of the drink. For a sour taste use lemon/lime, and for a sweet flavour, use coffee, chocolate or any other sweet liqueur. Hold the glass parallel to the table. Dab the rim into the dry agent like salt, sugar which can be coloured with food colorants, cocoa, shredded coconut, etc. Slowly turn the glass so that only the outer edge is covered. Shake off any excess dry agent before filling the glass with drink and garnish.

Any powdered, crumbled or granulated ingredient can be used as a rimmer. Cocoa powder is a great rimming option for chocolaty drinks.

Blending

Take a blender or else use crushed ice to blend. Place the ingredients into the blender cup. If the drink is fruit based, blend the fruit first, then add the crushed ice. Start blending at low speed and gradually increase to medium. Blend until smooth.

Tip: To keep the texture of the drink for a longer period of time, use a chilled glass.

Drink too thin: A big hole in the drink while blending indicates that the drink is too thin and some ice needs to be added.

Drink too thick: A drink not moving while blending means it is too thick and more juice needs to be added.

Perfect blend: When the drink moves with a little hole while blending, it means that the drink is blended perfectly.

Cocktails

VODKA

Plum Vodka Joy

Ingredients

Lime vodka **45 ml**
Plum liqueur **15 ml**
Custard apple purée, fresh **10 gm**
Vanilla sugar **5 gm**
Ice **6 cubes**
Pineapple juice **60 ml**

Method

Combine all the ingredients together in a cocktail shaker and shake thoroughly. Double strain the drink and pour into a glass. Serve.

Garnish Plum and vanilla pod
Glass Martini

Passionate

Ingredients
Vodka **30 ml**
Passion fruit liqueur **15 ml**
Midori* **15 ml**
Lemon juice, fresh **10 ml**
Sprite to top up

Method
Combine all the ingredients (except Sprite) together along with some ice in a cocktail shaker. Shake well and strain the drink into a tall glass. Top up with Sprite and serve.

Garnish Lemon slice and cherry
Glass Tom Collins

* Midori is a melon liqueur with a sweet, fruity taste.

Pink Macbeth

Ingredients
Vodka **50 ml**
Black grapes, fresh **10-15**
Rose syrup **25 ml**
Lemon juice, fresh **10 ml**
Rose petals for garnish

Method
Combine ice cubes and black grapes in a cocktail shaker. Pour premium vodka and rose syrup. Shake all the ingredients together. Double strain the drink and pour into a glass. Serve.

Garnish Rose petals
Glass Jazz

Guava Martini

Ingredients
Vodka **60 ml**
Apple juice **45 ml**
Lemon juice **10 ml**
Salt **a pinch**
Guava, fresh **1 slice**

Method
Combine all the ingredients along with some ice in a cocktail shaker and shake well. Pour the drink into a salt-rimmed glass and serve.

Garnish Guava slice
Glass Martini

Thyme Martini

Ingredients
Citrus vodka **50 ml**
Lemon marmalade **2 barspoons**
Thyme, fresh **3 sprigs**

Method
Muddle and shake all the ingredients together in a cocktail shaker. Pour the drink into a glass and serve.

Garnish Thyme sprig
Glass Martini

Cinnamon Martini

Ingredients
Cinnamon vodka **45 ml**
Pineapple, fresh **2 slices**
Fruit syrup **10 ml**
Lemon juice, fresh **10 ml**

Method
Muddle the pineapple slices with fruit syrup in a cocktail shaker. Add the cinnamon vodka along with some ice and shake well to mix. Strain the drink and pour into a chilled glass. Serve.

Garnish Vodka-soaked baked cinnamon stick
Glass Martini

Chazzle Dazzle

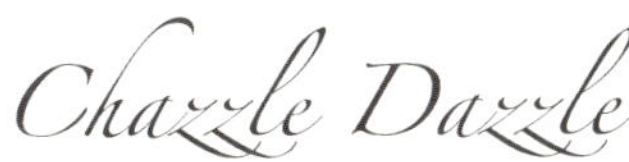

Ingredients
Vodka **45 ml**
Cucumber **2 slices**
Mint **6 leaves**
Lychee juice **75 ml**
Guava juice **60 ml**
Lemon juice, fresh **10 ml**
Crème de menthe* **15 ml**

Method
Muddle the cucumber slices with the mint leaves. Add the remaining ingredients (except crème de menthe) along with some ice cubes and stir well. Then finally, add the crème de menthe and pour the drink into a glass and serve.

Garnish Cucumber slice
Glass Tom Collins

* Crème de menthe is a sweet, mint-flavoured alcoholic beverage.

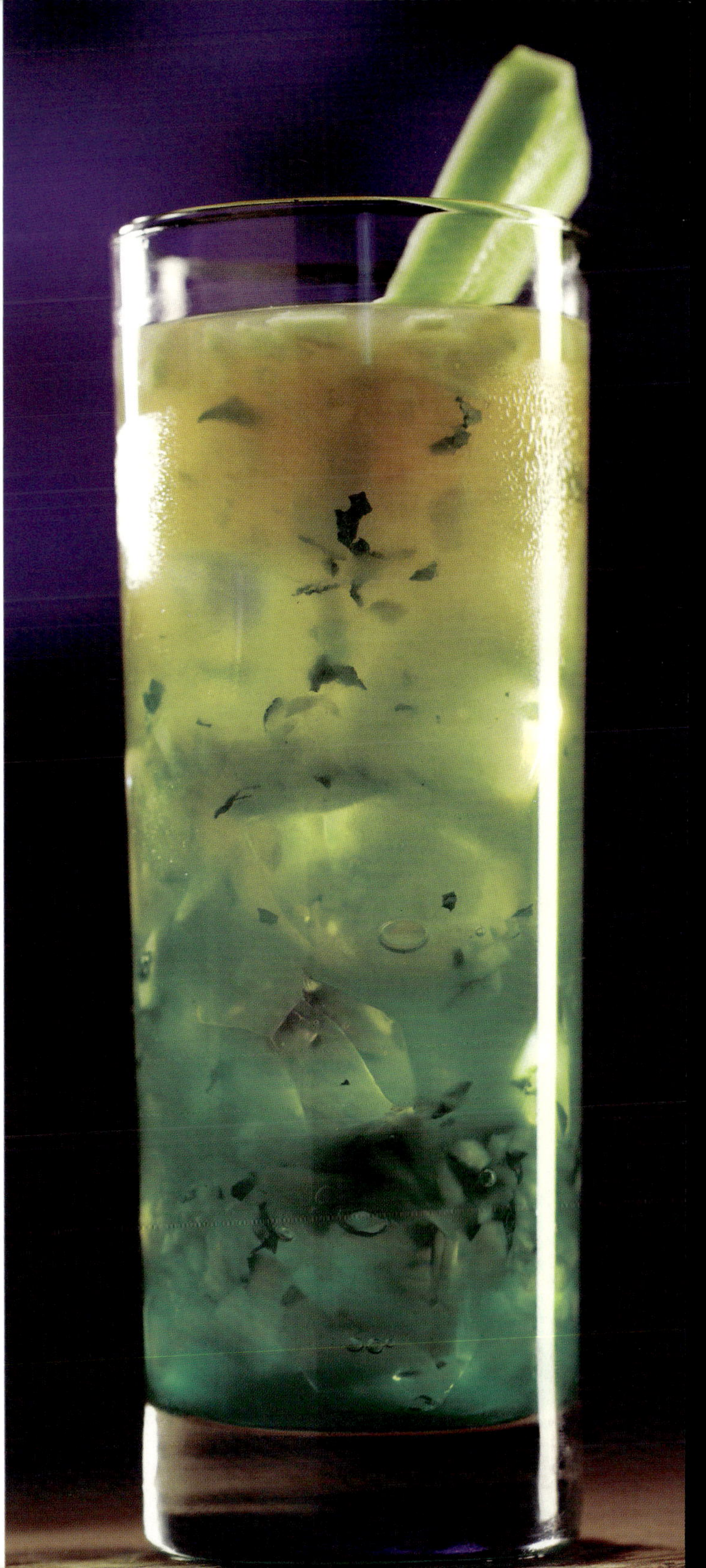

Flirtini

Ingredients
Vodka **45 ml**
Peach schnapps **15 ml**
Ginger juice **5 ml**

Method
Combine all the ingredients together along with some ice in a cocktail shaker. Shake well and strain the drink into a glass. Serve.

Garnish A peach slice
Glass Martini

Tokyo Drift

Ingredients
Vodka **45 ml**
Musk melon **5-6 chunks**
Mint **a sprig**
Midori **15 ml**
Lemon juice **10 ml**
Sprite to top up

Method
Muddle the musk melon and mint in a glass. Add the vodka, midori, and lemon juice. Top up with some ice cubes and Sprite. Serve.

Garnish A mint sprig
Glass Tom Collins

Lazy Suzanne

Ingredients

Mandarin vodka **45 ml**
Peach schnapps **15 ml**
Orange juice **60 ml**
Green apple juice **60 ml**
Cranberry juice **30 ml**

Method

Build all the ingredients together (except the cranberry juice) in a glass filled with ice. Float the cranberry juice on top and serve.

Garnish Green apple
Glass Hurricane

Rosemary Love

Ingredients
Vodka **60 ml**
Mandarin, fresh **1**
Rosemary, fresh **1 sprig**

Method
Muddle the mandarin and rosemary in an ice shaker. Add the vodka and shake with ice. Pour the drink into a chilled glass and serve.

Garnish Rosemary sprig
Glass Martini

Bhangra Time

Ingredients

Vodka **45 ml**
Tequila **15 ml**
Passion fruit syrup **5 ml**
Peach syrup **5 ml**
Apple syrup **5 ml**
Lemon juice **5 ml**

Method

Combine all the ingredients together along with some ice in a cocktail shaker. Shake well and strain the drink. Pour into a glass and serve.

Garnish Lemon slice
Glass Martini

Les Roches

Ingredients

White rum **30 ml**
Dark rum **30 ml**
Pineapple juice **45 ml**
Lemon slice for garnish

Method

Take a liquor glass and pour the white rum. Add the pineapple juice. Carefully pour the dark rum as it should not mix with the juice and white rum as it will float on the glass.

Garnish Lemon slice
Glass Cocktail

Saffron Breeze

Ingredients
Premium vodka **45 ml**
Whole sweet lime (juice) **1**
Lemon juice, fresh **10 ml**
Powdered sugar **2 tsp**
Ice **10-12 cubes**
Saffron **a pinch**

Method
Combine all the ingredients (except the saffron) together in a cocktail shaker and shake well. Double strain the drink and pour into a glass. Serve.

Garnish Saffron strands on top
Glass Martini

Babe on the Rocks

Ingredients
Vodka **30 ml**
Coffee liqueur **30 ml**
Cream to milk (2:1) **45 ml**
Cocoa powder to rim the glass

Method
Rim the glass with cocoa powder. Pour the coffee liqueur and vodka into a glass filled with ice. Float the cream and milk on top. Serve without stirring.

Garnish Cocoa-rimmed glass
Glass Old-fashioned

Bay Breeze

Ingredients
Vodka **60 ml**
Lemon juice **10 ml**
Triple sec **15 ml**
Champagne **50 ml**

Method
Pour the vodka, lemon juice, and triple sec over ice in a cocktail shaker. Shake well and strain the drink into a glass. Top up with champagne and serve.

Garnish Orange swirl
Glass Champagne flute

Orange Cranberry Martini

Ingredients

Vodka **30 ml**
Orange juice **30 ml**
Cranberry juice **45 ml**
Lemon juice **10 ml**
Sugar syrup **10 ml**

Method

Combine all the ingredients along with some ice in a cocktail shaker and shake well. Strain the drink into a chilled glass and serve.

Garnish Orchid
Glass Martini

Icy Spicy Blue

Ingredients

Vodka **80 ml**

Jalapeno juice **10 ml**

Blue curacao **5 ml**

Method

Combine the vodka and jalapeno juice in a cocktail shaker along with some crushed ice and shake well. Pour in the blue curacao. Strain the drink into a chilled glass and serve.

Garnish Jalapeno slice / Red chilli

Glass Martini

Hazelnut Caprioska

Ingredients

Vodka **45 ml**

Lemon **6 segments**

Hazelnut syrup **15 ml**

Method

Muddle the lemon segments with hazelnut syrup. Add the crushed ice and pour the vodka over the ice. Serve.

Garnish Mint sprigs

Glass Studio rock

Gari Blossom

Ingredients
Vodka **60 ml**
Lemon juice, fresh **15 ml**
Sugar syrup **15 ml**
Gari* **5 thin slices**

Method
Combine all the ingredients together in a cocktail shaker and shake well. Strain the drink and pour into a glass. Serve. Gari should be freshly infused in the vodka else it might give a bitter aftertaste.

Garnish Thin slices of gari
Glass Martini

* Gari is young ginger marinated in sugar and vinegar.

Wicked Touch

Ingredients
Vodka **45 ml**
Basil **3 leaves**
Cointreau **15 ml**
Orange tang **10 ml**
Orange juice, fresh **20 ml**

Method
Slightly muddle the basil leaves in a glass. Fill the glass with ice cubes and add the remaining ingredients, stir well and serve.

Garnish Orange slice
Glass Royale

Espresso Martini

Ingredients
Vodka **45 ml**
Coffee liqueur **15 ml**
Espresso **15 ml**
Sugar syrup **10 ml**

Method

Combine all the ingredients together along with some ice cubes in a cocktail shaker and shake well. Pour the drink into a chilled glass and serve.

Garnish Coffee beans
Glass Martini

Watermelon Caprioska

Ingredients
Vodka **60 ml**
Demerara sugar **1 tsp**
Mint, fresh **8 leaves**
Watermelon, fresh **4-5 cubes**
Lemon wedges **3 pieces**
Crushed ice **1 scoop**
7up / Sprite to top up

Method
Put the demerara sugar in a glass. Add the mint leaves, watermelon and lemon wedges. Muddle all the ingredients together. Add the vodka and top up with crushed ice and 7 up or Sprite. Serve.

Garnish Mint sprigs and small scoops of watermelon
Glass Old-fashioned

Shanghai Sunset

Ingredients
Vodka **30 ml**
Tequila **30 ml**
Pineapple juice **180 ml**
Cranberry juice **60 ml**
Ice
Chilli flakes

Method
Put all the ingredients into a mixing glass with ice, stir gently. Pour into a glass, which is rimmed with salt and chilli flakes (optional).

Garnish Lemon Slice
Glass Old-fashioned

Green Apple Martini

Ingredients
Vodka **45 ml**
Sour apple pucker **15 ml**
Lemon juice, fresh **5 ml**
Ice **10 cubes**

Method
Fill the cocktail shaker with ice cubes. Add the vodka, sour apple pucker and lemon juice. Stir properly with a stirrer. Double strain the drink into a glass and serve.

Garnish Green apple slice
Glass Martini

Punica Martini

Ingredients

Vodka **60 ml**
Pomegranate juice, fresh **60 ml**
Mint, fresh **1 leaf**
Lemon juice, fresh **15 ml**

Method

Muddle the pomegranate juice and mint leaf together. Add the vodka and lemon juice; shake well and serve.

Garnish Fresh basil leaf
Glass Martini

Caprioska Twisted

Ingredients

Vodka **60 ml**
Sweet lime **20 gm**
Lemon chunks **5 gm**
White sugar **20 gm**
Crushed ice
Soda **a dash**

Method

Muddle the sweet lime with lemon and sugar. Add vodka into the glass, crushed ice and a dash of soda on top.

Garnish Sweet lime slice
Glass Old-fashioned

Mango Rosemary Martini

Ingredients

Vodka **50 ml**
Rosemary **2 sprigs**
Martini Bianco* **10 ml**
Mango juice **45 ml**
Lemon juice, fresh **10 ml**
Sugar syrup **10 ml**
Crushed ice

Method

Gently muddle the rosemary and all the ingredients along with some ice in a cocktail shaker. Shake well and double strain the drink into a glass. Serve.

Garnish Rosemary sprig and lemon slice
Glass Martini

*Martini Bianco is a fine blend of Italian white wine infused with herbs. It produces an aromatic yet delicate drink with notes of vanilla and citrus. It is readily available.

Bejewelled

Ingredients
Vodka **30 ml**
Midori* **30 ml**
Sweet melon **50 gm**
Cream, fresh **60 ml**

Method
Pour Midori frappe in the base of the glass. Blend melon, vodka and cream together. Float the mixture on the frappe.

Garnish Pomegranate seeds
Glass Martini

* Midori is a melon liqueur with a sweet, fruity taste. It is readily available.

Mysterious Martini

Ingredients
Vodka **60 ml**
Smoked pineapple **5-6 cubes**
Vanilla pod
Ice cubes

Method
Muddle the pineapple in a cocktail shaker. Add vodka. Shake with ice and serve chilled in a chilled glass.

Garnish A smoked pineapple cube and vanilla pod (The fresh vanilla pod garnish doubles as a straw leaving a symphony of bitter fresh vanilla pod on the lips and hints of sweet vanilla on the palate).
Glass Martini

Here Comes the Bride

Ingredients
Vodka **30 ml**
Cointreau **15 ml**
Fruit & spice flavoured liqueur **15 ml**
Crushed ice

Method
Fill up a glass with finely crushed ice and add all the ingredients. Serve.

Glass Margarita

Blushing Damsel

Ingredients

Vodka **60 ml**
Lychee juice **60 ml**
Cranberry juice **60 ml**
Lemon juice **10 ml**
Lychees **3 pieces**
Crushed ice

Method

Shake the lychee juice, cranberry juice, lemon juice, and vodka in a shaker and pour over crushed ice into a glass.

Garnish Lychees on a toothpick
Glass Margarita coupe

Caprioska

Ingredients
Vodka **60 ml**
Lemon, cut into chunks **1**
Demerara sugar **1 sachet**
Crushed ice

Method
Muddle the lemon chunks in a rock glass with sugar. Add vodka and top with ice. Stir and serve.

Garnish Lemon wedge on the rim
Glass Old-fashioned

Sly Thai Martini

Ingredients
Vodka **60 ml**
Lychee juice **30 ml**
Lemon juice **a dash**

Method
Pour all the ingredients over ice into a shaker, shake vigorously and strain into a chilled glass.

Garnish Fresh lemon leaf
Glass Martini

Hallelujah

Ingredients
Vodka **60 ml**
Pineapple **4 slices**
Black pepper **a pinch**
Pineapple juice **30 ml**
Ice

Method
Grill the pineapple slices and muddle them along with black pepper. Pour the rest of the ingredients in a cocktail shaker with ice and shake until chilled. Double strain into a chilled glass.

Glass Martini

Be My Valentine

Ingredients
Vodka **45 ml**
Pomegranate **7 chunks**
White sugar **1 tsp**
Lemon, cut into slices **1**
Sweet and sour mix **15 ml**

Method
Muddle the pomegranate chunks, white sugar, and lemon slices with sweet and sour mix. Top up with vodka.

Garnish Lemon wedge
Glass Old-fashioned

Velvet Kimono

Ingredients

Vodka **60 ml**
Watermelon, fresh **4-5 chunks**
Watermelon syrup **10 ml**
Lemon juice **5 ml**
Ice

Method

Muddle the fresh watermelon chunks with watermelon syrup in a mixing glass. Add lemon juice and vodka with lots of ice, shake well and fine strain into a chilled glass.

Garnish Watermelon balls
Glass Martini

Oriental Spice

Ingredients

Vodka **60 ml**
Guava juice **150 ml**
Worcestershire sauce **4 drops**
Tabasco sauce **2-3 drops**
Lemon juice **5 ml**
Ice
Chilli flakes

Method

Put all the ingredients in a mixing glass with ice, stir gently and pour into a salt and chilli flake-rimmed glass.

Garnish Lemon slices
Glass Old-fashioned

Rambagh Polo

Ingredients
Vodka **45 ml**
Triple sec **10 ml**
Melon purée **60 ml**
Lemon juice **10 ml**
Melon **10 pieces**

Method
Put all the ingredients in a cocktail shaker, shake and pour into a glass.

Garnish Lemon slice
Glass Highball

Bartender's Affair

Ingredients
Vodka **60 ml**
Peach schnapps **15 ml**
Cranberry juice **15 ml**
Lemon juice, fresh **10 ml**
Ice cubes

Method
Mix vodka, peach schnapps, cranberry juice, fresh lemon juice, and ice together.

Garnish Lemon Swirl
Glass Martini

Tikitini

Ingredients

Vodka **60 ml**
Lemon grass **5-6 sprigs**
Lemon juice, fresh **10 ml**
Martini (Dry/Sweet) **10 ml**
Sugar syrup **5 ml**

Method

Muddle the lemon grass in a mixing tin with the help of a muddler and keep aside. Fill a cocktail shaker with ice and add the remaining ingredients along with the muddled lemon grass, shake well, and double strain the drink into a glass. Serve.

Garnish Lemon grass stick
Glass Martini

Ingredients

Vodka **45 ml**
Triple sec **15 ml**
Lemons, cut into wedges **2**
Ice cubes

Method

Put all the ingredients into a shaker. Shake well. Strain into a Chilled glass.

Garnish Lemon wedge
Glass Cocktail

Peach Dew

Ingredients
Vodka **45 ml**
Peach schnapps **15 ml**
Peach tea **90 ml**

Method
Take a cocktail shaker. Add 30 ml vodka along with peach schnapps and peach tea. Pour into a glass.

Garnish Flame the remaining vodka and float on the drink
Glass Martini

Cafetini

Ingredients
Vodka **45 ml**
Irish cream whiskey **15 ml**
Coffee liqueur **15 ml**
Coffee decoction **30 ml**
Chocolate syrup for rimming

Method
Put chocolate syrup in a glass and swirl it around the glass. Shake all the ingredients together in a shaker and pour into a glass.

Garnish Chocolate stick
Glass Martini

Apple Delight

Ingredients
Vodka **60 ml**
Green apple syrup **15 ml**
Apple juice **45 ml**
Green apple **1 slice**

Method
Add the green apple syrup, vodka, ice cubes, and top up with apple juice. Garnish with apple slice.

Garnish Apple slice and mint sprigs
Glass Old-fashioned

Coffee Delight

Ingredients
Vodka **60 ml**
Single espresso
Ice cubes

Method
Shake the vodka and espresso with ice and serve in a sugar-rimmed glass.

Garnish Coffee beans
Glass Martini

RUM

Minty Mojito

Ingredients

Rum (your favourite) **50 ml**
Lemon, quartered **1 piece**
Mint leaves **8-10 sprigs**
Demerara sugar **2 sachets**
Cucumber **2 slices**
Sprite / 7up to top up
Rock salt **a dash**

Method

Squeeze the lemon quarters into a high ball glass and drop the lemons into the glass. Add mint leaves and sugar. Place cucumber round slices into the glass and fill with ice. Pour in the rum and top up with Sprite/ 7up.

Garnish Diced cucumber and mint leaves
Glass Tom Collins

Kiwi Martini

Ingredients
Spiced rum **60 ml**
Kiwi, fresh **1 slice**
Apple juice **45 ml**
Lemon juice **10 ml**
Sugar **1 sachet**

Method
Put all the ingredients together with ice in a shaker and shake well. Rim the glass with sugar.

Garnish Kiwi slice
Glass Martini

Watermelon Panther

Ingredients
White rum **60 ml**
Watermelon chunks **6-8 chunks**
Mint leaves **4-5 sprigs**
Demerara sugar **to taste**
Lemon juice **1 tsp**
Sprite / 7up to top up

Method
Muddle watermelon chunks, mint leaves, and demerara sugar together to extract the mint and watermelon flavour. Then add a few drops of lemon juice and rum with crushed ice and then top up with Sprite / 7up.

Garnish Watermelon slice
Glass Cooler

Glow in the Dark

Ingredients
White rum **30 ml**
Tequila **30 ml**
Malibu **10 ml**
Blue curacao **15 ml**
Lemon juice **5 ml**
Sprite / 7up to top up
Crushed ice

Method
Pour all the ingredients in the glass, add crushed ice and stir.

Garnish Lemon slice
Glass Tom Collins

Dark Temptation

Ingredients
Dark rum **20 ml**
Italian anise-flavoured liqueur **20 ml**
Coffee liqueur **20 ml**
Ice cubes

Method
Put all the ingredients in a cocktail shaker. Shake with ice and strain into a glass.

Garnish Coffee beans
Glass Martini

Port of Spain

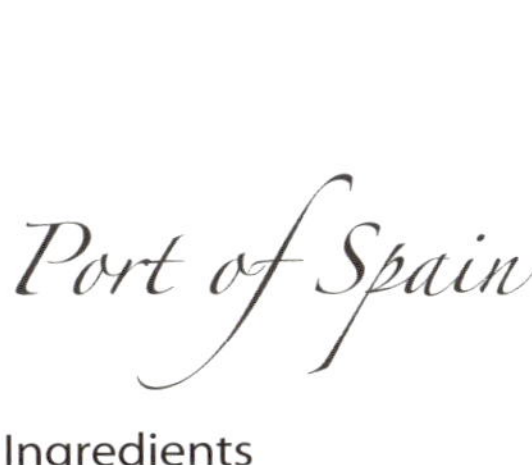

Ingredients

Caribbean rum **60 ml**
Apple **6 chunks**
Apple juice **60 ml**
Ginger **2 gm**
Homemade vanilla sugar
(sugar mix of vanilla pods) **10 gm**
Pear purée **10 gm**
Ice cubes

Method

Muddle apple, apple juice, and ginger together with vanilla sugar. Add pear purée to the mixture. Shake with ice cubes and Angostura rum. Pour into a glass with ice.

Garnish Apple slice
Glass Tom Collins

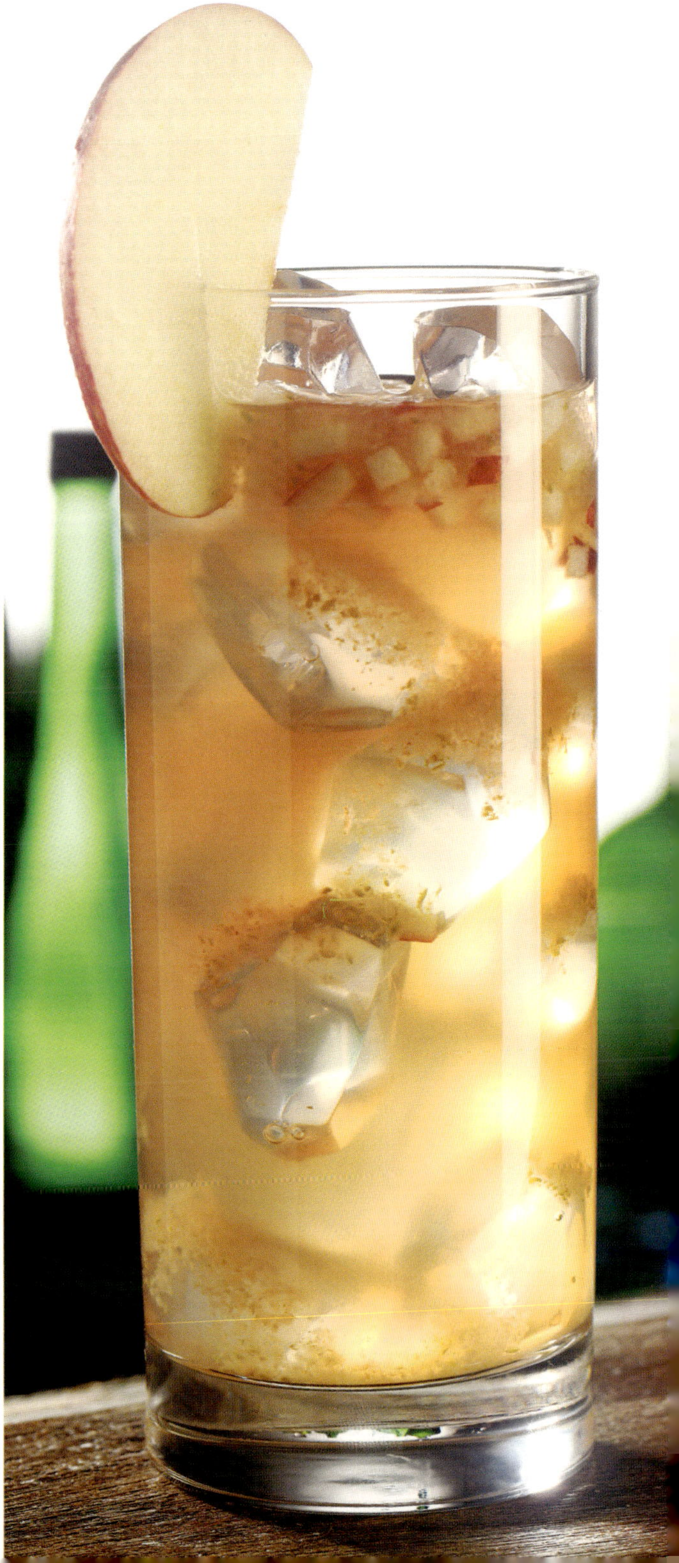

Coconut Punch

Ingredients
White rum **60 ml**
Lemon juice **10 ml**
Coconut sliced **4**
Coconut tender **1**

Method
Pour all the ingredients in a cocktail shaker with ice. Shake well and pour into a chilled glass.

Garnish Coconut slice
Glass Martini

Fresh Sweet Lime Mojito

Ingredients
Light Rum **60 ml**
Fresh sweet lime **4 chunks**
Lemon **2 wedges**
Mint **6 leaves**
Soda to top up
Crushed ice

Method
In a shaker add all the ingredients except the rum. Muddle it nicely, pour into a royal highball glass. Add crushed ice and rum. Top up with a dash of soda.

Garnish Lemon slice
Glass Royal highball

Kuebano

Ingredients
Dark premium rum **45 ml**
Cranberry juice **60 ml**
Fresh lemon juice **15 ml**
Ice cubes

Method
Shake all the ingredients in a shaker. Pour over rock ice.

Garnish Lemon slice
Glass Highball

Mojito Royale

Ingredients
White rum **45 ml**
Sparkling wine **60 ml**
Mint **3-4 sprigs**
Ginger **2-3 chunks**
Lemon **5-6 wedges**
Simple syrup **15 ml**
Crushed ice

Method
Muddle mint, ginger, lemon wedges with simple syrup. Add crushed ice and white rum. Stir then top up with sparkling wine.

Garnish Mint sprigs
Glass Cocktail

Go Banana

Ingredients
Dark rum **30 ml**
Irish cream whiskey **30 ml**
Crème de banana **30 ml**

Method
Blend all the ingredients with crushed ice. Pour in a glass. Serve chilled.

Garnish Caramelised banana
Glass Margarita

Taxi Call

Ingredients

Dark rum **30 ml**
Light rum **30 ml**
Brandy **15 ml**
Peach juice **30 ml**
Crème de banana* **10 ml**
Triple sec **5 ml**
Grenadine** **5 ml**
Orange juice **60 ml**
Pineapple juice **60 ml**
Crushed ice

Method

Mix all the ingredients with crushed ice. Serve chilled.

Garnish Orange wheel
Glass Pilsner

* Crème de banana is a sweet, banana-flavoured liqueur
** Grenadine is traditionally a red syrup. It is used as an ingredient in cocktails, both for its flavour and to give a reddish / pink tinge to mixed drinks.

Cuban Chill

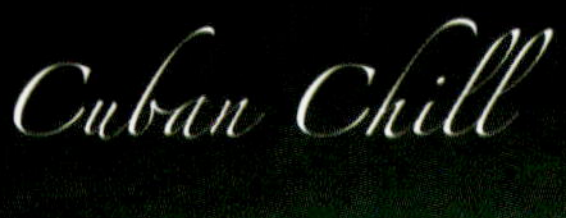

Ingredients

White rum **45 ml**
Triple sec **15 ml**
Lemon juice **30 ml**
Almond syrup **15 ml**
Rose water **5 drops**
Ice cubes

Method

Shake all the ingredients into a cocktail shaker and pour into a glass with ice.

Garnish Caramelised almond and orange zest
Glass Old-fashioned

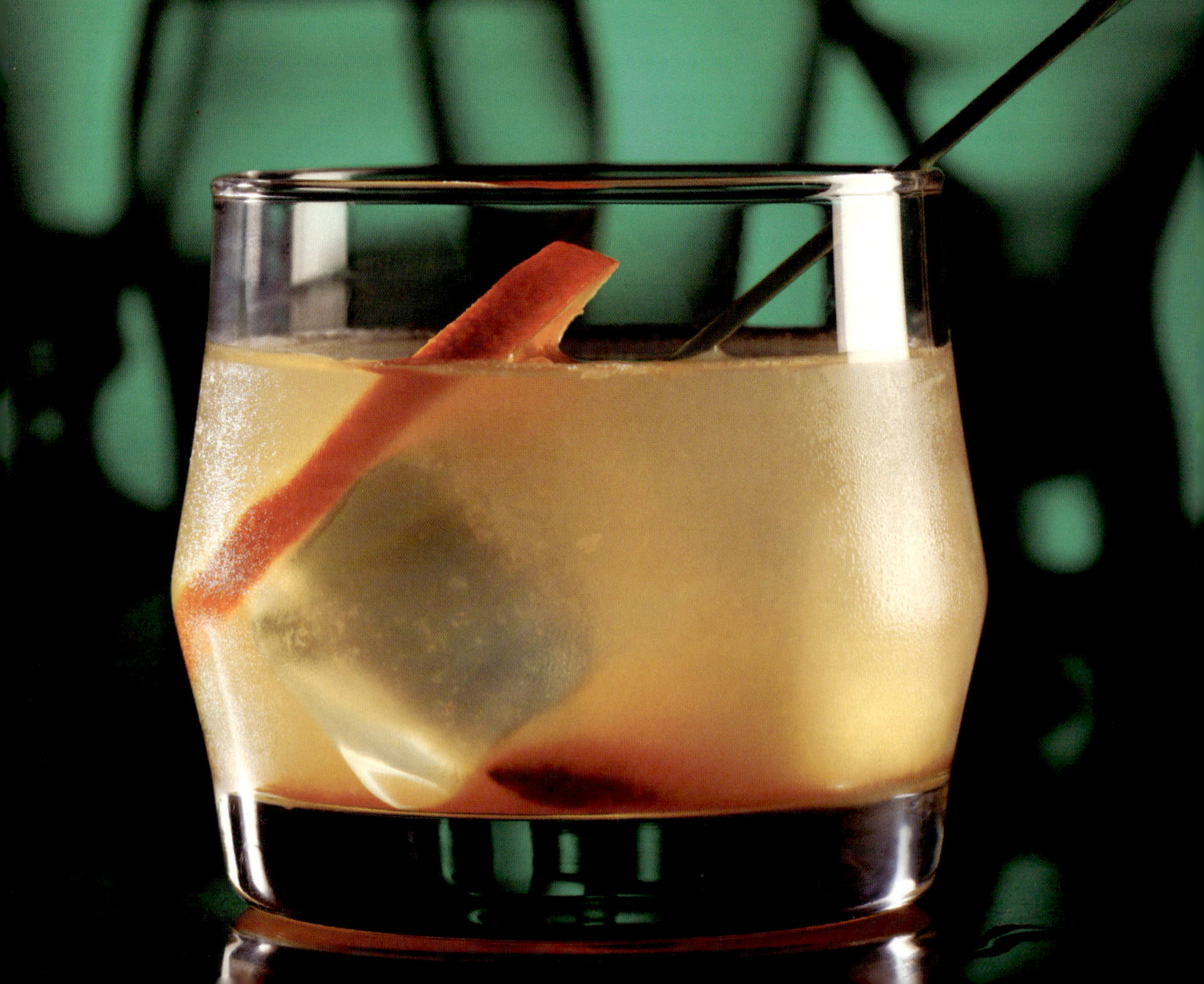

Star's Illusion

Ingredients
Cuban 7 years rum **45 ml**
Star fruit **1**
Fenugreek seeds **2 barspoons**
Lychee juice **30 ml**
Monin orgeat syrup* **10 ml**
Ice cubes

Method
In a mixing glass, put fenugreek seeds and star fruit and muddle. Add ice, rum, lychee juice, and Monin orgeat syrup, shake and double strain into a glass.

Garnish Star fruit slice
Glass Martini

* Monin Orgeat (Almond) Syrup features the natural, true almond flavour.

Summer Blossom

Ingredients
White rum **60 ml**
Orange juice, fresh **250 ml**
Orange slices **20 gm**
Grenadine **5 ml**
Ice cubes

Method
Layer the slices of orange with ice. Add grenadine. Add rum and orange juice into the glass.

Garnish Orange wedge or mint leaves
Glass Tom Collins

Raging Bull

Ingredients

White rum **30 ml**
Gold rum **30 ml**
Amaretto **10 ml**
Pineapple **4 slices**
Pineapple juice **30 ml**
Orange **2 slices**
Orange juice **30 ml**
Ice cubes

Method

Muddle the grilled pineapple and orange slices with orange and pineapple juice. Pour the rum and amaretto along with the muddled ingredients in a cocktail shaker with ice and shake.

Garnish Roasted pineapple and orange. Float dark rum on top.
Glass Tom Collins

Apple and Basil Mojito

Ingredients

White rum **60 ml**
Green apple **6-8 chunks**
Basil **8-10 leaves**
Brown sugar **1 tsp**
Green apple syrup **15 ml**
Lemon juice **10-15 ml**
Cracked ice

Method

Muddle apple chunks and basil leaves with brown sugar in an old-fashioned glass. Pour apple syrup, lemon juice, and white rum in the glass. Add cracked ice and soda.

Garnish Basil leaves and apple slice
Glass Old-fashioned

Apple Seduction

Ingredients

White rum **60 ml**
Lemon **6 wedges**
Mint **8 leaves**
Sugar **2 sachets**
Apple **4 slices**
Apple juice **90 ml**
Cracked ice

Method

Muddle lemon wedges and mint with sugar in the glass. Top the glass with cracked ice. Add four quarter slices of apple to the glass, and white rum. Top up with apple juice.

Garnish Mint leaf
Glass Studio Rock

Orange Splash

Ingredients

White rum **60 ml**
Mint leaves **5 sprigs**
Orange **2 wedges**
Lemon juice **15 ml**
Orange juice **90 ml**
Soda water **a splash**
Orange **1 slice**
Crushed ice

Method

Lightly muddle the mint leaves with orange wedges and lemon juice. Add rum and orange juice. Top with crushed ice and soda water. Stir well to mix all the flavours.

Garnish Orange swirl
Glass Old-fashioned

The Secret Garden

Ingredients

White rum **60 ml**
Green apple syrup **10 ml**
Mint **5-6 leaves**
Caster sugar **1 barspoon**
Lemon **4 wedges**
Lemon juice **10 ml**

Method

Squeeze lemon wedges into a glass. Add all the ingredients, muddle it gently. Add crushed ice and white rum, mix well and top up with more ice.

Garnish Mint sprigs, lemon slice and chopped apple.
Glass Old-fashioned

Hibiscus and Vanilla Daiquiri

Ingredients
Rum **60 ml**
Vanilla syrup* **20 ml**
Strong hibiscus tea** **60 ml**
Lemon **2 pieces**
Sugar syrup **5 ml**

Method
In mixing glass, add all the ingredients and ice. Shake and double strain into a glass.
Garnish Hibiscus flower and vanilla pod
Glass Old-fashioned

* To make Vanilla Syrup: Slice 6 vanilla sticks. Remove vanilla beans and drop beans and pods into a saucepan. Add 1 bottle of mineral water and 1 cup of sugar; boil for 15 minutes. Pour all the ingredients into a bottle and refrigerate.
* * To make Hibiscus Tea: Buy some nice Hibiscus tea, place 8 Hibiscus flowers with 1 bottle of water in a saucepan and boil for 15 minutes. Strain the flowers away keeping a few for garnishing. Pour the remaining tea into a bottle and refrigerate.

Mandarin Sour

Ingredients

White rum **45 ml**
Green kiwi, peeled **¼**
Lemon, cut into thin wedges **⅓rd**
Mint **6 leaves**
Ice cubes

Method

Put the kiwi, lemon slices, and mint leaves in a tall glass and muddle. Fill ⅔rd of the glass with ice. Add rum and stir. Top up with club soda and stir again.

Garnish Kiwi slice and mint leaves
Glass Highball

Liquid Tiramisu Shot

Ingredients

English cream infused with Amaretto **45 ml**
Espresso infused with dark rum **30 ml**
Whipped cream **15 ml**

Method

In a shot glass layer English cream then espresso and the whipped cream and serve chilled.

Garnish Coffee dust
Glass Shot

Blueberry Mojito

Ingredients

White rum **60 ml**
Lemon **5-6 wedges**
Mint **15-18 leaves**
Blueberry syrup **20 ml**
Blueberries **5-6 pieces**
Sprite to top up
Ice cubes

Method

Take a cocktail shaker and add 10 cubes of ice. Add 4 lemon wedges with 15 mint leaves and blueberry syrup; muddle them. Add rum and top up with Sprite. Shake well and pour into a glass.

Garnish Lemon wedges, mint and blueberries
Glass Tall glass

Spicy Coco

Ingredients

Rum **45 ml**
Lemon juice **a dash**
Coriander leaves **3 sprigs**
Chilli **1 piece**
Coconut water to top up
Ice cubes

Method

Take a shot glass and add few cubes of ice. Add rum and lime juice with coriander leaves. Top up with coconut water.

Garnish Green Chilli & Coriander leaves
Glass Shot

Mango Mojito

Ingredients

White rum **60 ml**
Lemon juice **15 ml**
Mint **8 leaves**
Brown sugar **1½ tsp**
Crushed ice **6 spoons**
Soda **30 ml**
Mango juice, fresh **15 ml**

Method

Muddle lemon juice, brown sugar, mint leaves, and a few mango chunks in a glass. Add crushed ice, mango juice, rum and top up with soda.

Garnish Mango slice and mint leaves
Glass Old-fashioned

Kerala Beauty

Ingredients

White rum **60 ml**
Pineapple juice **30 ml**
Cream, fresh **5 ml**
Coconut liqueur **10 ml**
Crushed ice

Method

Mix white rum with pineapple juice, fresh cream, coconut liqueur, and crushed ice. Pour into a glass.

Garnish Pineapple slice and mint sprigs
Glass Highball

Killer by the Beach

Ingredients
Vodka **30 ml**
White rum **15 ml**
Italian anise-flavoured liqueur **10 ml**
Tender coconut water **120 ml**
Sugar syrup **30 ml**
Tonic water to top up
Ice cubes

Method
Pour all the ingredients (except tonic water) over ice in a mixing tin. Shake and strain into a glass filled with ice. Top with tonic water.

Garnish Lemon slice, cherries, mint sprigs
Glass Pilsner

Isabella

Ingredients
White rum **60 ml**
Californian grapes **2-3**
Sweet 'n' sour mix **5 ml**
Grape juice **60 ml**
Apple juice **15 ml**
Crushed ice

Method
Muddle grape chunks in an old-fashioned/ rock glass with sweet 'n' sour mix, pour in the white rum. Fill the glass with crushed ice, top up with grape and apple juice.

Garnish California grapes
Glass Old-fashioned or rock glass

Mango Madorita

Ingredients

Premium Cachaça Brazilian rum **60 ml**
Lemon juice **10 ml**
Mango purée **120 ml**
Mint **6 leaves**
Crushed ice

Method

Pour all the ingredients together in a blender with ice. Blend and pour into a glass.

Garnish Cherries
Glass Margarita

WHISKEY

Cigar Smoked Julep

Ingredients

Bourbon Whiskey **60 ml**
White sugar **10 gm**
Mint, fresh **6 sprigs**

Method

Muddle sugar and mint together. Then add Bourbon whiskey. Shake with crushed ice. Pour into a glass and add smoke with a smoking gun. This tool quickly and effortlessly infuses foods and drinks with natural smoky flavours without the extra heat.

Garnish Mint sprigs
Glass Old-fashioned

Boom-e-Rang

Ingredients
Whiskey **60 ml**
Raspberry purée **1½ tsp**
Cranberry juice **60 ml**
Lemon juice **10 ml**
Sugar syrup **a dash**
Ice cubes

Method
Put all the ingredients together with ice in a shaker and shake well. Strain and serve.

Garnish Lemon slice
Glass Tall

Just Like That

Ingredients
Whiskey **60 ml**
Passion fruit syrup **20 ml**
Pineapple juice **120 ml**
Lemon juice **a dash**
Crushed ice

Method
Shake the whiskey, passion fruit syrup, and pineapple juice in a shaker full of ice. Strain in a glass.

Garnish Lemon spiral
Glass Tom Collins

Heaven and Hell

Ingredients
Vodka **30 ml**
Tennesse Whiskey **15 ml**
Peach schnapps **15 ml**
Pineapple juice **30 ml**
Orange juice **60 ml**
Grenadine **5 ml**
Lemon juice **5 ml**
Crushed ice

Method
Shake all the ingredients; mix well with crushed ice. Pour in the glass.

Garnish Red cherries
Glass Wine

Love Bite

Ingredients
Vodka **30 ml**
Fruit & spice flavoured liqueur **30 ml**
Crème de cassis **15 ml**
Orange juice **100 ml**
Ice cubes

Method
Put two cubes of ice in a glass. Pour vodka, the liqueur and crème de cassis. Top up with orange juice. Stir and serve.

Garnish Orange and cherries
Glass Old-fashioned

Dark side of You

Ingredients

Tennesse Whiskey **45 ml**
Pouring cream **30 ml**
Dark chocolate syrup **30 ml**
Crème de menthe **10 ml**
Whipped cream **½ cup**

Method

Shake the whiskey, pouring cream, and dark chocolate syrup well. Line the glass with a dash of crème de menthe beaten with whipped cream. Pour the mixture into the glass.

Garnish Chocolate flakes
Glass Champagne flute

Kiwi Mojito

Ingredients
Bourbon whiskey **45 ml**
Sweet 'n' sour mix **15 ml**
Mandarin juice **30 ml**
Kiwi **1 Chopped**
Crushed ice

Method
Muddle 2 table spoon chopped kiwi in a shaker with 8 to 10 ice cubes, add Bourbon whiskey, sweet n sour mix, mandarin juice shake well pour over crushed ice.

Garnish Mandarin zest
Glass Old-fashioned

Siamese Sour

Ingredients
Whiskey **45 ml**
Orange liqueur **30 ml**
Orange juice **60 ml**
Lemon juice, fresh **15 ml**
Lemon **1 wedge**
Ice cubes

Method
Take a cocktail shaker and add 10 cubes of ice. Add all the above ingredients and shake well. Pour into a glass.

Garnish Lemon wedge
Glass Martini

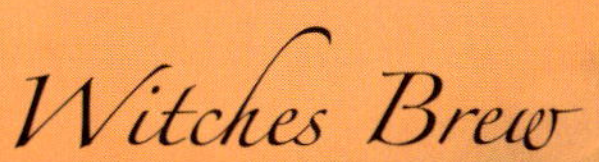

Ingredients

Irish cream whiskey **30 ml**
Coffee liqueur **15 ml**
Vodka **30 ml**
Sugar syrup **a dash**
Ice cubes

Method

Add all the ingredients in the blender with ice cubes. Blend and pour into a glass.

Garnish Lemon spiral
Glass Martini

Mint Julep

Ingredients
Bourbon whiskey **60 ml**
Mint **5-6 sprigs**
Simple syrup **15 ml**
Crushed ice

Method
Muddle mint with simple syrup. Add crushed ice and bourbon whiskey. Stir and serve.

Garnish Mint sprigs
Glass Old-fashioned

Tiramisu

Ingredients
Bourbon whiskey **45 ml**
Coffee liqueur **15 ml**
Single cream **15 ml**
Crushed ice

Method
Pour the whiskey in a glass. Put the liqueur in it with the help of back side of long barspoon. Add crushed ice. Top up with single cream.

Garnish Coffee rimmed glass and coffee beans
Glass Old-fashioned

Drambuie Sour on the Rock

Ingredients
Drambuie* **60 ml**
Lemon juice **10 ml**
Egg white **optional**
Ice cubes

Method
Line up lemon wheels at the bottom of a glass. Put loads of ice. Shake Drambuie and lemon juice together, strain the liquid into the glass.

Garnish Lemon wheels
Glass Martini

* Drambuie is a sweet, golden coloured 80-proof liqueur made from malt whisky, honey, herbs, and spices.

Flaming Lamborghini

Ingredients

Irish cream whiskey **30 ml**
Coffee liqueur **30 ml**
Italian anise-flavoured liqueur **30 ml**
Blue curacao **30 ml**

Method

Pour the anise-flavoured and coffee liqueur into a cocktail glass. Add the Irish cream whiskey and blue curacao into two separate shot glasses and keep on either side of the cocktail glass. Set alight the concoction in the cocktail glass and start drinking through a straw. As the bottom of the glass is reached put out the fire by pouring the whiskey and blue curacao into the cocktail glass and keep drinking till it's all gone.

Glass Cocktail

WINE

Black Beauty

Ingredients
Red wine **150 ml**
Brandy **30 ml**
Angostura bitter* **5 drops**
Cinnamon stick **1 piece**
Brown sugar to rim the glass

Method
Rim the red wine glass with brown sugar. Flame and caramelise the glass with half of the brandy. Put the red wine, angostura bitter and cinnamon stick, flame the leftover brandy and put the flaming brandy on top.

Garnish Brown sugar-rimmed glass
Glass Brandy balloon

* Angostura Bitter is made from a secret blend of rare tropical herbs and spices.

Citrus Sangria

Ingredients
White wine **120 ml**
Citrus vodka **15 ml**
Lemon **4 slices**
Orange **1**
Sugar syrup **15 ml**
Lemon juice **15 ml**
Orange juice **30 ml**
Strawberry for garnish
Ice cubes

Method
Pour all the ingredients in a Boston shaker with 4 cubes of ice and mix well. Pour into a wine glass and serve.

Garnish Orange and strawberry slice
Glass Wine

Jade Fizz

Ingredients
Sparkling wine **120 ml**
Crème de menthe **30 ml**
Cherries or blue berries or strawberry **2**

Method
Pour crème de menthe in a champagne flute and top up with sparkling wine.

Garnish Any berry
Glass Champagne flute

Veda

Ingredients
Champagne or
sparkling wine **150 ml**
Cherry liquor **15 ml**
Cherries for garnish

Method
Pour sparkling wine in a tulip. Float cherry liquor on top.

Garnish Cherries
Glass Champagne tulip

Cabernet Cobbler

Ingredients
Red wine **90 ml**
Lemon juice **10 ml**
Sugar syrup **10 ml**
Soda water **40 ml**
Crushed ice

Method
Mix lemon juice and sugar syrup with red wine, pour over ice and top up with soda water.

Garnish Lemon slice
Glass Wine

Fly High!

Ingredients

White wine **60 ml**
Crème de cassis* **15 ml**
Malibu** **10 ml**
Coconut crème **a dash**
Ice cubes

Method

Add ice cubes and all the ingredients in a shaker. Shake well and strain into a glass.

Garnish Cherry and lemon slice
Glass Chilled margarita

* Crème de cassis is a blood-red, sweet, black currant-flavoured liqueur.
** Malibu has its own strong dominant flavour and the chilled white wine adds to the distinct coolness to the drink.

Forbidden Fruit

Ingredients
Sweet white wine **90 ml**
Pomegranate **½ cut**
Lemon juice **a dash**
Cinnamon **1 stick**
Passion fruit liquor **15 ml**
Sugar syrup **10 ml**
Ice cubes

Method
Take a handful of pomegranate seeds, bruise it with dash of lemon juice, sugar syrup, and cinnamon stick. Put passion fruit liquor and mix well. Pour into a glass. Load the glass with ice. Float the wine in the glass. Stir the mixture.

Garnish Fresh mint sprig
Glass Pilsner

Shiraz Sangria

Ingredients
Red wine **1 bottle** (preferably young, light body Shiraz wine)
Lemon **1** (cut into wedges 1x6)
Orange **1** (cut into wedges 1x6)
Sugar **2 tbsp**
Brandy **1 shot**
Ginger ale or club soda **2 cups**

Method
Pour wine in the pitcher and squeeze the juice from the lemon and orange wedges into the wine. (squeeze 2 lemon and 2 orange wedges each) Toss in the rest of fruit wedges leaving out seeds if possible and add sugar and brandy. Chill overnight, so that the wine absorbs the flavours of the fruits. Add ginger ale or club soda just before serving.

Garnish Orange slice
Glass Large wine glass

Blue Bamboo

Ingredients

White wine **90 ml**
Gin **30 ml**
Blue curacao **15 ml**
Lemonade to top up
Ice cubes

Method

Pour the gin and white wine in a tall glass. Add 2 cubes of ice and top up with lemonade. Float the blue curacao on it and serve.

Garnish Lemon slice
Glass Tall

Hemingway

Ingredients

French anise-flavoured liqueur **30 ml**
Champagne **150 ml**

Method

Pour the liqueur in a champagne flute glass and top up with champagne.

Garnish Star anise
Glass Champagne

GIN

Kaffir Sapphire

Ingredients

Premium gin **60 ml**
Lemon grass simple syrup **15 ml**

Method

Shake the gin and simple syrup with ice till the outside frosts. Strain into a serving glass.

Garnish Kaffir lemon leaf
Glass Martini

Sizzling Lady

Gin **60 ml**
Lychee crush **15 ml**
Lemon juice **10 ml**
Sugar syrup **10 ml**
Grenadine syrup **5 drops**
Soda to top up
Crushed ice

Method

Put lychee crush, gin, lemon juice, and sugar syrup in a shaker. Shake it with crushed ice. Pour the mixture into the glass, put soda and grenadine on top.

Garnish Lemon slice
Glass Hurricane

Saffron Martini

Ingredients

Premium gin **50 ml**
Dry vermouth **10 ml**
Saffron **5 strands**
Ice cubes

Method

Immerse the strands of saffron in 10 ml of warm water beforehand so as to release the colour and flavour.

Shake the gin and vermouth in a cocktail shaker with lots of ice. Strain in a chilled glass. Release about 4-5 drops of saffron water over the martini and leave 1 strand of saffron in the drink for garnish.

Garnish Saffron strand
Glass Cocktail

Ice Berg

Ingredients
Gin **60 ml**
Crème de menthe **15 ml**

Method
Stir the gin and liqueur with ice in a shaker till the outside frosts. Strain into a serving glass.

Garnish Mint sprig
Glass Martini

Japanese Melon

Ingredients
Gin **60 ml**
Watermelon, fresh **6-8 chunks**
Kaffir **3 leaves**
Lemon **1 piece**

Method
Muddle kaffir leaves and watermelon.
Add gin and a squeeze of lemon juice; shake well.
Pour into a glass.

Garnish Watermelon cubes
Glass Old-fashioned

Salmon Catch

Ingredients
Smoked salmon infused dry gin* **50 ml**
Sauvignon Blanc **15 ml**
Capers **3 pieces**
Milk powder **½ packet**
Lemon **1 piece**
Ice cubes

Method
In a mixing glass, gently muddle capers.
Add ice, ½ packet milk powder, lemon juice. Add gin and wine, shake and double strain into a glass.

Garnish Lemon rings
Glass Martini
*To make smoked salmon infused gin place a few pieces of smoked salmon in a jar with dry gin. Refrigerate for 24 hours, then strain away the smoked salmon.

Coriander Flame

Ingredients

Wine **60 ml**
Coriander, fresh **1 sprig**
Ginger, fresh **1 slice**
Cucumber, fresh **1 slice**
Angostura bitter **2 drops**
Soda **a dash**
Ice cubes

Method

Muddle all the fresh ingredients. Pour Hendricks over ice. Add a dash of soda.

Garnish Cucumber slice
Glass Old-fashioned

Blushing Darling

Ingredients

Plum infused gin **60 ml**
Californian plum, fresh **1 piece**
Ice cubes

Method

Muddle the plum in a mixing glass. Add the infused gin and mix. Pour the drink over ice in a glass and serve.

Garnish Plum slice
Glass Highball

Pink City Classic

Ingredients

Gin **60 ml**

Rose syrup **4 ml**

Martini rose **2**

Crème de fraise **2 ml**

Method

Add all the ingredients into a cocktail shaker, shake and pour into a glass.

Garnish Cherry and mint sprig

Glass Cocktail

Poolside Fetish

Ingredients

Gin **45 ml**
Cherry brandy **15 ml**
Benedictine **10 ml**
Triple sec **10 ml**
Angostura bitter **a few drops**
Grenadine syrup **15 ml**
Pineapple juice **150 ml**
Ice cubes

Method

Pour all the ingredients in Boston shaker. Fill the glass with ice cubes and shake well.

Garnish Pineapple
Glass Pilsner

Muay Thai

Ingredients
Gin **45 ml**
Lychees (fresh / canned) **2**
Lemon juice **5 ml**
Lychee juice (fresh / canned) **60 ml**
Crushed ice

Method
Put alternate layers of crushed ice, slightly bruised kaffir leaves and lychee halves in a glass. Add lemon juice, lychee juice, and gin to top the drink. Serve with a cocktail stirrer.

Garnish Lemon slice with kaffir leaves
Glass Tall

COGNAC

Jynnx

Ingredients
Orange liqueur **15 ml**
Almond liqueur **15 ml**
Cognac **30 ml**
Vanilla ice cream **1 scoop**
Crushed ice

Method
Blend briefly all the ingredients together with half a glass of crushed ice, pour into the high ball glass. Garnish with a wedge of orange.

Garnish Wedge of orange
Glass Highball

Cigar Lovers' Martini

Ingredients
Cognac **74 ml**
Port wine **15 ml**
Ice cubes

Method
Fill ¾th of a shaker with ice, add the above ingredients and shake vigorously. Strain in a chilled martini glass.

Garnish Orange swirl
Glass Martini

Barista

Ingredients
Cognac **45 ml**
Irish whiskey **15 ml**
Freshly Brewed Coffee **30 ml**
Demerara Sugar (Brown) **1 tsp**
Whipped Cream **2 tsp**

Method
Take a wine glass and rub the rim with honey and Demerara Sugar. Add Cognac and Irish whiskey. Then add 1 tsp sugar and dissolve it. Pour freshly brewed coffee and add whipped cream.

Garnish Coffee Beans
Glass Wine

Devil in You

Ingredients
Cognac **45 ml**
Fresh strawberries **5**
Vanilla ice cream **one scoop**
Milk **30 ml**
Coconut syrup **15 ml**
Ice cubes

Method
Take a blender and add 6 cubes of ice. Put fresh strawberries, ice cream, milk, coconut syrup, and cognac. Make it like a smoothie.

Garnish Fresh strawberry
Glass Tulip

Airstrike

Ingredients
Galliano* **2 measures**
Cognac **1 measure**
Star anise **1 piece**

Method
Mix Galliano and cognac in a cocktail glass. Flambé with star anise for approximately 50 seconds. Cool and serve.

Garnish star anise
Glass Martini or Cocktail

* Galliano is a sweet herbal liqueur.

Dead Revival

Ingredients
Cognac **30 ml**
Apple brandy **20 ml**
Sweet Red Vermouth **10 ml**
Ice cubes

Method
Pour ingredients into a cocktail shaker, fill it with ice cubes. Stir well. Strain into a chilled martini glass.

Garnish Maraschino cherry
Glass Martini

Tordie

Ingredients
Cognac **60 ml**
Lukewarm water **80 ml**
Honey **A teaspoon**
Fresh Lemon **15 ml**
Crushed Cloves **1**

Method
Pour Cognac in a Brandy Snifter.
Add lukewarm water. Add a teaspoon of Honey, 15ml fresh lemon, 1crushed clove. Stir well before serving.

Garnish Lemon wedge
Glass Brandy Snifter

Cognac Ginger Hail

Ingredients
Cognac **45 ml**
Ginger ale **120 ml**
Lemon peel **Several strands**
Sugar syrup **15 ml**
Cucumber peel **2 strips**
Ice cubes to fill glass

Method
Muddle the lemon peel and cucumber peel in the glass very gently. Add the ice and Cognac & Sugar syrup, Stir and top with ginger ale.

Garnish Ginger slice
Glass Highball

Clove Cinnamon Partner

Ingredients
Cognac **60 ml**
Lemon juice **15 ml**
Honey **15 ml**
Cinnamon powder **¼ spoon**
Clove powder **¼ spoon**
Hot Water **120 ml**

Method
Mix cognac, lemon juice, honey, cinnamon powder and clove powder in brandy balloon glass. Top it up with hot water.

Garnish Cinnamon powder rimmed glass
Glass Brandy balloon

Alexander

Ingredients
Cognac **45 ml**
Fresh Cream **60 ml**
Crème de Cacao **15ml**
Cinnamon Powder **a pinch**

Method
Put in all ingredients in a shaker that is half-filled with ice. Shake well and pour it in the cocktail glass. Sprinkle with Cinnamon before serving.

Garnish Cinnamon powder
Glass Martini or Cocktail

Banana Bliss

Ingredients
Cognac **60 ml**
Crème de Banane **30 ml**
Ice **2 cubes**
Cherries for garnish

Method
Put two ice cubes and the other ingredients into a mix glass. Stir and pour into a tumbler glass.

Garnish Cherries
Glass Tumbler

Red Sleeper

Ingredients

Cognac **60 ml**
Brown sugar **½ tsp**
Mint **8-10 leaves**
Apple juice **15 ml**
Cranberry juice **30 ml**
Lemon juice, fresh **10 ml**
Ice cubes

Method

Muddle the brown sugar and mint leaves in a glass. Add some ice and then pour the remaining ingredients; stir well and serve.

Garnish Mint sprigs
Glass Brandy Balloon

Espresso Sidecar

Ingredients

Cognac **45 ml**
Triple sec **15 ml**
Espresso **15 ml**
Sugar syrup **15 ml**
Lemon juice **15 ml**
Ice cubes

Method

Shake all the ingredients together with ice in a cocktail shaker and pour into a glass.

Garnish Coffee bean and lemon slice
Glass Martini

Winter Met

Ingredients

Cognac **45 ml**
Dark liqueur with coffee flavour **15 ml**
Ginger ale syrup **10 ml**

Method

Pour cognac, the liqueur, and ginger ale syrup in a shaker without ice. Stir it well.

Glass Brandy balloon

TEQUILA

Tequila Sunrise

Ingredients
Tequila **60 ml**
Orange juice **120 ml**
Grenadine syrup **10 ml**
Ice cubes

Method
Add orange juice, tequila, and grenadine syrup over ice cubes. Stir and serve.

Garnish Orange slice
Glass Highball

Hot Fire on the Rocks

Ingredients
Tequila **60 ml**
Cranberry juice **90 ml**
Lemon juice **15 ml**
Sugar syrup **10 ml**
Ice cubes

Method
Mix all with ice and serve in salted rim old-fashioned glass.

Garnish Lemon wedge
Glass Old-fashioned

Kiwi Margarita

Ingredients

Tequila silver **45 ml**
Kiwi liquor **14 ml**
Sweet n sour mix **30 ml**
Kiwi, peeled **1 (cut into cubes)**
Crushed ice

Method

Take crushed ice, tequila, kiwi liquor, sweet and sour mix, and 1 fresh kiwi (cut into cubes) in a blender. Blend for 2 minutes.

Garnish Kiwi slice
Glass Margarita

Tequila Basil Exotica

Ingredients

Tequila **45 ml**
Cointreau **15 ml**
Basil **5 leaves**
Black peppercorns **4**
Lemon juice **15 ml**
Sugar syrup **15 ml**
Ice cubes

Method

Muddle basil leaves and black peppercorns. Add lemon juice, sugar syrup, tequila, and Cointreau. Shake all the ingredients well with ice and strain into a glass.

Garnish Basil leaves
Glass Martini

Soul Happiness

Ingredients

Camino silver tequila **60 ml**
Fresh squeezed lemon juice **20 ml**
Watermelon simple syrup **30 ml**
Ice cubes

Method

Shake all the ingredients hard over ice, and strain into a chilled glass.

Garnish Watermelon slice
Glass Martini

Lemon Paradise

Ingredients

Tequila **45 ml**
Cointreau **15 ml**
Lemon juice **10 ml**
Sugar syrup **10 ml**
Ice cubes

Method

Put all the ingredients in a blender along with ice. Blend and pour in a Margarita glass rimmed with salt.

Garnish Lemon slice
Glass Margarita

Mr Suave

Ingredients
Tequila **40 ml**
Orange vodka **20 ml**
Orange juice **30 ml**
Simple sugar syrup **1 barspoon**
Crushed ice

Method
Pour all the ingredients into a cocktail shaker and add crushed ice. Leave for 5 seconds and shake well. Fine strain into a rock glass.

Garnish Pineapple and mint
Glass Studio rock

Lolita

Ingredients
Tequila **60 ml**
Lemon juice, fresh **10 ml**
Kiwi purée **60 ml**
Lemon drink of your choice **60 ml**
Crushed ice

Method
Combine all the ingredients together (except the lemon drink) in a cocktail shaker and shake well. Pour the drink over crushed ice in a glass. Top up with the lemon drink.

Garnish Kiwi slice
Glass Cocktail

Savoy Royal

Ingredients

Tequila **60 ml**
Kiwi **2 Slices**
Strawberry **2 pieces**
Lemon Juice **10 ml**
Sugar Syrup **10 ml**
Ice cubes

Method

Blend together 30ml tequila, kiwi slices, 5ml lemon juice and 5ml sugar syrup with ice & pour in margarita glass. Separately, blend together 30ml tequila, strawberries, 5ml lemon juice and 5ml sugar syrup with ice & layer it on top. Garnish with kiwi slice.

Garnish Kiwi slice
Glass Margarita

MIXED ALCOHOL

Tall Guy

Ingredients
Gin **30 ml**
Vodka **30 ml**
Tequila **30 ml**
White rum **30 ml**
Triple sec **30 ml**
Lemon juice **30 ml**
Coke to top up

Method
Take a long glass and fill it up with ice. Pour vodka, gin, tequila, white rum, triple sec, and lemon juice; stir. Top up with coke.

Garnish Lemon slice
Glass Tall

Walk on the Moon

Ingredients
Vodka **15 ml**
Gin **15 ml**
Tequila **15 ml**
White rum **15 ml**
Peach liqueur **15 ml**
Orange juice **60 ml**
Cranberry juice **60 ml**
Ice cubes

Method
Pour all the ingredients in a shaker along with lots of ice and shake well. Serve with some ice.

Garnish Orange slices
Glass Tall

Oh It's Kahlua!

Ingredients
Italian anise-flavoured liqueur **15 ml**
Irish cream whiskey **15 ml**
Kahlua **15 ml**
Cinnamon stick
Ice cubes

Method
Build all the ingredients in a roly-poly glass with 4 cubes of ice.

Garnish Cinnamon stick
Glass Roly poly

Pretty Senorita

Ingredients

Coconut or cashew feni **60 ml**
Lemon juice **60 ml**
Strawberry crush **5 ml**

Method

Shake all the ingredients and serve in a sugar-rimmed margarita glass.

Garnish Slit strawberries
Glass Margarita

Lovely Green

Ingredients

Shochu* **30 ml**
Sweet and sour mix **15 ml**
Cucumber purée **30 ml**
Medori** **15 ml**
Ice cubes

Method

Muddle all the ingredients in a cocktail shaker with ice. Shake well and serve.

Garnish Cucumber peel
Glass Martini

* Shochu is a Japanese clear distilled spirit similar to vodka.
** Midori is a melon liqueur with a sweet, fruity taste.

Little Ninza

Ingredients
Taru sake* **40 ml**
Malibu **20 ml**
Melon syrup **5 ml**
Blue Curacao **a dash**
Cherries for garnish
Ice cubes

Method
Pour all the ingredients over ice into a shaker, shake vigorously and strain into rock glass.

Garnish Red cherries
Glass Rock

* Taru Sake is a typical dry Japanese sake characterised by its refreshing taste and the wooden aroma of Yoshino cedar.

Sake may be substituted by shochu to make a stronger drink.

Thunderstruck

Ingredients
Absinthe* **30 ml**
Jagermeister** **30 ml**
Champagne **150 ml**

Method
Pour Absinthe and Jagermeister in a champagne flute. Top up with champagne.

Garnish Orange rind
Glass Stemless Champagne flute

* Absinthe is a high alcohol volume (usually 50-70%) licorice-flavoured herbal liqueur.
** Jägermeister (hunt master) is a German bitter liqueur that is a complex blend of 56 herbs, fruits and spices.

Royal Passion

Ingredients
Cachaça **60 ml**
Passion fruit purée **10 ml**
Lemon juice **10 ml**
Sugar syrup **15 ml**
Crushed ice

Method
Muddle all the ingredients in a tall glass.
Top up with crushed ice.

Garnish Lemon wedge
Glass Tom Collins

Brunch Blast

Ingredients
Cachaça **60 ml**
Triple Sec 2 **15 ml**
Freshly squeezed lemon juice **15 ml**
Guava nectar **120 ml**
Ice cubes

Method
Shake Cachaça, triple sec, lemon juice, guava nectar with ice and pour into a serving glass.

Garnish Kiwi Slice
Glass Cocktail

This is the Night!

Ingredients

Cachaça* **60 ml**
Demerara sugar **10 gm**
Basil, finely chopped **5 leaves**
Lemon juice **10 ml**
Sweet lime juice (optional) **30 ml**
Watermelon (seedless) **5 cubes**
Crushed ice

Method

Muddle together cachaça, sugar, basil, and lime juices. Pour the mixture over the watermelon and let it soak overnight in the refrigerator. Blend all the ingredients and pour into a glass on crushed ice.

Garnish Watermelon cube
Glass Tom Collins

* Cachaça or "Ca-SHAH-sa" is a liquor made from fermented sugarcane juice. It is the most popular distilled alcoholic beverage in Brazil.

Chak de Phatte

Ingredients
Gin **10 ml**
White Rum **10 ml**
Vodka **10 ml**
Tequila **10 ml**
Cointreau **10 ml**
Blue Curacao **5 ml**
Dark rum **10 ml**
Whiskey **10 ml**
Sprite **1 can**
Lemon chunks **8nos**
Lemon juice **10 ml**
Sugar syrup **10 ml**
Ice cubes

Method

Take lemon chunks in shaker and muddle them. Pour all the white spirits in a brandy embassy glass along with sugar syrup and lemon juice. Fill the glass with ice cubes and top it up with sprite and pour blue Curacao. Float dark spirits on top of it for a layering.

Garnish Lemon slice
Glass Old-fashioned

Asian Politan
Ingredients
Sake 60 ml
Cointreau 15 ml
Lemon juice 10 ml
Cranberry juice 15 ml
Crushed ice
Method
Fill a mixing glass with crushed ice, lemon juice and all the ingredients. Shake well. Serve the drink in a chilled Martini glass.
Granish Orange slice
Glass Martini

Mind Wash

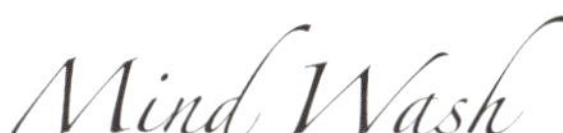

Ingredients
Vodka **15 ml**
Cachaça **15 ml**
Gin **15 ml**
Tequila **15 ml**
Blue Curacao **15 ml**
Fresh lemon juice **10 ml**
Lemonade to top up
Ice cubes

Method
Shake all the ingredients together with ice and pour into a glass. Top up with lemonade.

Garnish Lemon slice
Glass Tom Collins

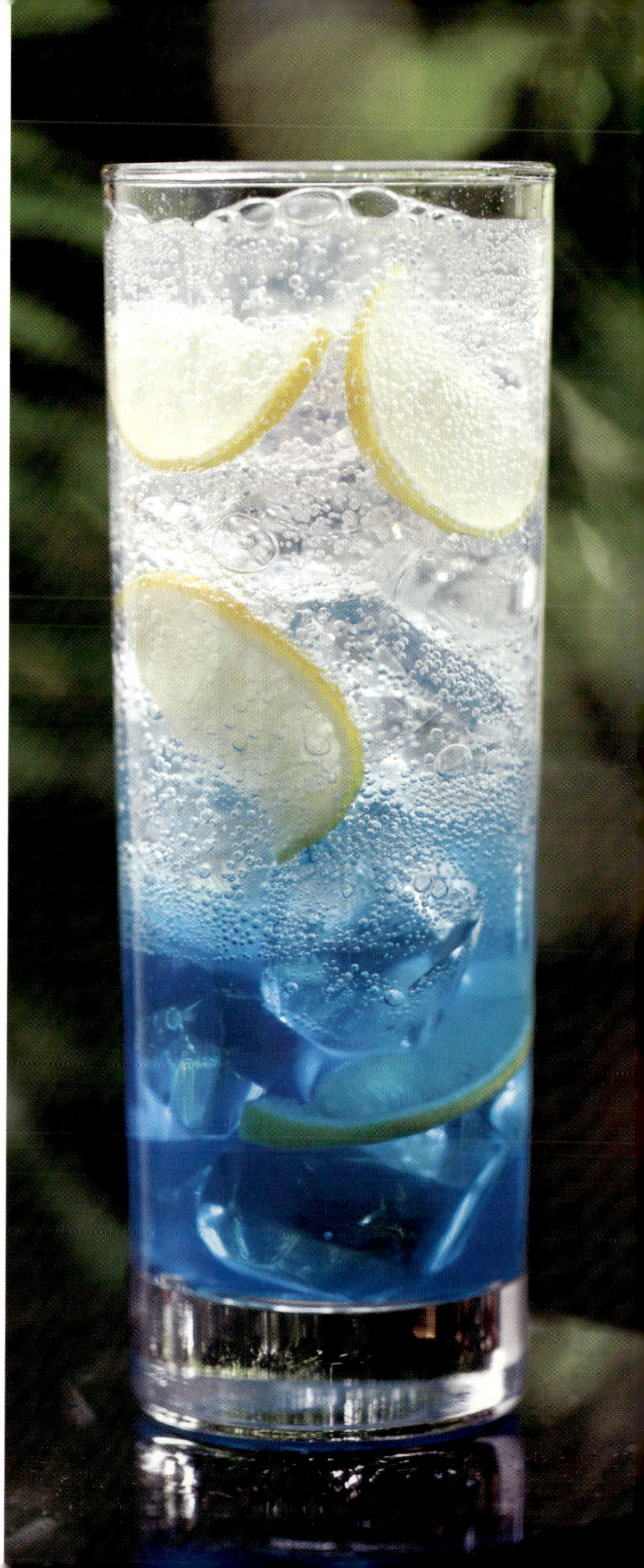

3 Ms - Melon Mint Martini

Ingredients
Stolichnaya* **60 ml**
Melon **6 pieces**
Martini Bianco** **2 ml**
Crème de menthe **3 ml**

Method
Add all the ingredients to the cocktail shaker, shake and pour into a glass.

Garnish Mint leaves
Glass Cocktail

* Stolichnaya is a Latvian vodka made of wheat and rye grain.
** Martini Bianco is a fine blend of Italian white wine infused with herbs and sweet floral botanicals and produces an aromatic yet delicate drink with notes of vanilla and citrus.

Oreo and Almond Sundae

Ingredients

Butterscotch ice cream **50 ml**
Fig and Honey ice cream **50 ml**
Oreo cookie **1 piece**
Caramelised almonds **15 gms**
Amaretto Liqueur **5 ml**
Whipped cream **10 gms**
Vanilla sauce **15 ml**

Method

Mix a scoop of each of the ice creams and add the crushed cookie.

Garnish Caramelised almonds, Amaretto liqueur and vanilla sauce
Glass Pilsner

Fizzi Gal

Ingredients

Vanilla ice cream **1 cup**
Chocolate syrup **¼ cup**
Milk **¾ cup**
Irish cream whiskey

Method

Pour all ingredients (Irish cream whiskey to taste) into a blender until smooth. Pour into a glass and serve immediately in a Pina Colada Glass.

Garnish Cinnamon powder rimmed glass
Glass Pina Colada

Spiced Cocktails

Masala Mary

Ingredients
Vodka **60 ml**
Chaat masala **10 gm**
White sugar **10 gm**
Tomato juice**150 ml**
Lemon juice **5 ml**
Worcestershire sauce **4-5 drop**
Ice cubes

For the tempering
Olive oil **30 ml**
Curry leaves **3-4**
Whole dry red chilli **1**
Mustard seeds **1 tsp**

Method
Rim the highball glass with chaat masala and white sugar mixture. Add 7-8 ice cubes in the glass. Add the vodka, tomato juice, lemon juice, and Worcestershire sauce. Temper the whole spices and curry leaves with olive oil and pour over the drink with a bit of olive oil.

Garnish Tempered spices and dash of olive oil
Glass Highball

Banaras

Ingredients
Gin **60 ml**
Fennel seeds **1 tsp**
Green cardamoms **3**
Dried betel leaves **a few**
Sugar syrup **5 ml**
Silver leaf **1**

Method
In a cocktail shaker muddle the fennel seeds, green cardamoms and dried paan. Add gin. Shake all the ingredients and fine strain in a chilled glass.

Garnish Silver leaf
Glass Martini

The Great Indian Masala Trick

Ingredients
White rum **60 ml**
Cumin powder **½ tsp**
Cardamom powder **½ tsp**
Black pepper powder **½ tsp**
Mango panna **30 ml**
Mace flower **1**

Method
Shake all the ingredients (except the mace flower) in a cocktail shaker and fine strain into a chilled glass.

Garnish Mace flower
Glass Martini

Spicy Sangria

Ingredients

Nutmeg **1 piece**
Star anise **1 piece**
Green cardamoms **2 pieces**
Red wine **120 ml**
Cinnamon infused vermouth **10 ml**
Honey **5 ml**
Apple, chopped **10 gm**
Pineapple, chopped **10 gm**
Plum, chopped **10 gm**
Ice cubes

Method

In a cocktail shaker, gently muddle all the spices. Add red wine, vermouth, and honey. Shake all the ingredients with ice and serve with ice.

Garnish Chopped fruits
Glass Old-fashioned

Kama-Summer Paradise

Ingredients

Tequila **60 ml**
Green chillies **2**
Lemon chunks **8-10 pieces**
Cinnamon syrup **15 ml**
Cinnamon bark for garnish
Crushed ice

Method

Build up on a bed of crushed ice in a lowball glass.

Garnish Cinnamon bark
Glass Lowball

As Night Falls

Ingredients
Vodka **60 ml**
Watermelon, fresh **4 chunks**
Simple syrup **15 ml** (1 part sugar added to 1 part boiled water. Once sugar is dissolved completely, left to cool.)
Freshly squeezed Lemon **½ pc**
Black pepper **a pinch**
Melon, scoops for garnish
Lemon slice for garnish
Ice cubes

Method
Place all the ingredients into a cocktail shaker filled with ice. Shake well and strain into a chilled glass.

Garnish Melon ball
Glass Martini

Sunny Riser

Ingredients

Vodka **45 ml**
Cloves or thyme **5 cloves or 15 leaves approx**
Gin **15 ml**
Orange juice **20 ml**

Method

Pour all the ingredients in a cocktail shaker. Shake well and strain into a chilled glass.

Garnish orange slice with thyme or cloves
Glass Martini

American Twister

Ingredients
Tennesse whiskey **60 ml**
Pink peppercorns **8**
Red wine vinegar **10 ml**
Apple juice **15 ml**

Method
Pour all the ingredients in a cocktail shaker. Double strain in a chilled glass.

Garnish Apple slice
Glass Martini

Porto Flip

Ingredients
Brandy **30 ml**
Port wine **45 ml** (preferably Six Grapes)
Simple syrup **8 ml**
Egg **1**
Whole nutmeg, freshly grated for garnish

Method
Add brandy, port, and simple syrup to a cocktail shaker. Add egg (yolk and white). Shake vigorously for a minute. Strain into a glass.

Garnish Grated nutmeg
Glass Old-fashioned

Med Wild Guava

Ingredients
Pepper vodka **60 ml**
Guava juice **120 ml**
Salt **a pinch**
Oregano **a pinch**
Rosemary **a pinch**
Lime juice **10 ml**
Black pepper **a pinch**
Red chilli flakes **a pinch**
Tabasco **3 drops**
Ice cubes

Method
Mix all the ingredients and pour into a celery salt-rimmed glass with ice.

Garnish Celery salt-rimmed
Glass Old-fashioned

Fire & Ice

Ingredients
Infused green chilli vodka **45 ml**
Lemon juice **15 ml**
Tabasco sauce **10 ml**
Sprite to top up
Ice cubes

Method
Mix all the ingredients. Add ice cubes, top up with Sprite.

Garnish Green chilli and cherry
Glass Pilsner

Strangular

Ingredients

Infused chilli vodka* **30 ml**
Mango juice **90 ml**
Tabasco **a few drops**
Dried red chilli **1**
Ice cubes

Method

Put some ice cubes in a cocktail shaker. Pour mango juice and chilli vodka. Shake and Strain into a chilled glass. Add few drops of Tabasco.

Garnish Dried red chilli
Glass Margarita

* Vodka can be infused by adding slit green chilies into the bottle. This prevents it from getting spoilt. The older it is kept the better it tastes.

Asian Muse

Ingredients

Lime vodka **60 ml**
Ginger ale **1 can**
Lemon grass **20 sprigs**
Kaffir lime leaves **20 sprigs**
Galangal **1 gm**

Method

Muddle all the ingredients together and pour into a glass.

Garnish Kaffir lime leaves
Glass Tom Collins

The Crowne Betel

Ingredients
Vodka **60 ml**
Cinnamon powder **1 tbsp**
Aniseed powder **1 tbsp**
Betel **5 leaves**

Method
Muddle all the ingredients together and pour into a glass.

Garnish Beetel leaves
Glass Beer pilsner

Mumbai Pantini

Ingredients
Smirnoff red **50 ml**
Sambuca vaccari* **10 ml**
Gulkhand **1 tsp**
Star anise powder **a pinch**
Betel **2 leaves**
Ice cubes

Method
Muddle the gulkhand and star anise powder. Add vodka and sambuca, pour into a cocktail shaker with ice; shake well and pour into a glass.

Garnish Betel leaf
Glass Martini

* Sambuca vaccari is a sweet, strong liqueur produced by alcohol extraction of the two types of anise: Mediterranean anise and Chinese star anise.

Teekha Peru

Ingredients
Smirnoff red **60 ml**
Lemon juice **10 ml**
Tabasco sauce **3 drops**
Guava juice **120 ml**
Salt **a pinch**
Red chilli powder to rim the glass
Green chilli **1**
Ice cubes

Method
Rim the glass with salt and red chilli powder. Add ice, pour in lemon juice, Tabasco sauce, guava juice, and a pinch of salt. Float vodka on top.

Garnish Chilli
Glass Hurricane

Chilli Coriander Martini

Ingredients
Vodka **60 ml**
Sweet and sour mix **30 ml**
Green chilli, fresh **1**
Coriander **4 leaves**
Chaat masala **a pinch**
Ice cubes

Method
Pour vodka, sweet and sour mix, and green chilli over ice into a shaker. Shake vigorously, strain into a chilled glass. Add a pinch of Chat masala and serve.

Garnish Coriander leaf
Glass Martini

Wasabi Martini

Ingredients
Vodka **60 ml**
Kiwi crush **a dash**
Wasabi paste
Ice cubes

Method
Pour all the ingredients over ice into a shaker, shake vigorously and strain into a glass.

Garnish Kiwi slice
Glass Martini

Spiced Monk

Ingredients

Dark rum **60 ml**
Galangal **3 chunks**
Lemon **2 chunks**
Lychee crush **30 ml**
Crushed ice

Method

Put galangal and lemon in a shaker. Muddle well. Pour into a glass. Add crushed ice, rum, and lychee crush. Stir and serve.

Garnish Lemon wheel
Glass Cocktail

Envy

Ingredients

Dark premium rum 23yrs **50 ml**
Lychee juice **60 ml**
Mango panna **15 ml**
Kaffir lime **2 leaves**
Lemon squeeze **1**
Ice cubes

Method

Put all the ingredients with ice in a mixing glass and shake. Double strain into a coupe glass.

Garnish Kaffir lime leaf
Glass Coupe

Ingredients
White rum **60 ml**
Chaat masala **a dash**
Lemon juice **a dash**
Sugar syrup **a dash**
Green apple syrup **15 ml**
Ice cubes

Method
Pour all the ingredients in a shaker with ice cubes. Shake well and pour into a frosted glass.

Garnish Apple slice
Glass Martini

Rum Cinnamon Tango

Ingredients
Dark rum **45 ml**
Cardamoms **2**
Star anise **1**
Whole cloves **6**
Apple juice **20 ml**
Apple **1**
Orange peel **1-6**
Cinnamon sticks **2**

Method
Take all the ingredients other than dark rum and boil all the spices with apple juice for approximately 3 minutes. Strain and pour into the glass. Add the dark rum and stir lightly.

Garnish Orange peel with cinnamon stick
Glass Old-fashioned or Irish cup

Guava Zini

Ingredients
Vodka **60 ml**
Guava juice **120 ml**
Red chilli powder **½ tsp**
Chaat masala powder **½ tsp**
Guava wedge **1**
Ice cubes

Method
Put ice, vodka and guava juice in a cocktail shaker and shake. Add red chilli powder and chaat masala, shake well. Strain and serve in chaat masala rimmed glass.

Garnish Guava wedge
Glass Old-fashioned

Durbar Mojito

Ingredients
Light rum **60 ml**
White sugar **2 barspoons**
Mint **8-10 leaves**
Curry leaves **6**
Ginger julienned **8-10**
Lemon segments **1½**
Soda to top up
Crushed ice

Method
Put sugar, mint leaves, curry leaves, ginger, and lemon wedges in a jazz glass. Muddle well, add the rum and stir. Put crushed ice and top with soda. Serve.

Garnish Mint sprig
Glass Jazz

Springly Smash

Ingredients

Scotch whisky **60 ml**
Mint, fresh **5-6 leaves**
Lemon juice **15 ml**
Sugar syrup **5 ml**
Soda to top up
Ice cubes
Lemon grass, fresh for garnish

Method

Mix whisky, mint leaves, lemon juice, sugar syrup, and ice cubes in a tall glass. Top up with soda.

Garnish Lemon grass and mint leaves
Glass Tom Collins

The Dual Jewel

Ingredients
Whisky **60 ml**
Guava juice **60 ml**
Grenadine syrup **10 ml**
Mint leaves **4 leaves**
Lemon juice **5 ml**
Green chilli **1**
Ice cubes

Method
Shake whisky, guava juice, grenadine syrup, mint leaves, and lemon juice together with ice.

Garnish Green chilli
Glass Martini

Angel on Horseback

Ingredients
Vodka **45 ml**
Apple juice **240 ml**
Cinnamon stick **2**
Honey **15 ml**
Cloves **2**
Ice cubes

Method
Boil apple juice with cinnamon stick, honey, and cloves. Remove and keep aside to cool. Then refrigerate. Pour vodka, flavoured apple juice and ice in a shaker. Shake and strain into a glass.

Garnish Cinnamon stick
Glass Martini

Mocktails

Déjá vu

Ingredients

Peach purée **15 ml**
Strawberry purée **15 ml**
Apricot purée **15 ml**
Ginger extract **5 ml**
Pineapple juice **90 ml**
Crushed Ice

Method

Shake all the ingredients with crushed ice and pour into a glass.

Garnish Pineapple slice
Glass Cocktail

Frost Byte

Ingredients

Green apple purée **15 ml**
Apple juice **60 ml**
Pear purée **15 ml**
Ginger extract **5 ml**
Ginger ale **1 can**
Crushed ice

Method

Mix all the ingredients with crushed ice and top up with ginger ale.

Garnish Ginger juliennes
Glass Pilsner

Bull Tail

Ingredients
Lemon chunks **9 pcs**
Mint leaves **15 sprigs**
Peach and
ginger syrup **10 ml each**
Red bull **1 can**
Ice cubes

Method
Muddle all the ingredients with ice and serve.

Garnish Lemon chunks and mint leaves
Glass Beer pilsner

Jack Sparrow

Ingredients
Spiced pumpkin purée **200 gm**
Mixed spices **cinnamon, cardamom, star anise, cloves**
Condensed milk **15 ml**
Crushed ice

Method
Bake the pumpkin with whole spices (cinnamon, cardamom, star anise, cloves) and muddle to purée. Shake with condensed milk and crushed ice.

Garnish Star anise
Glass Margarita

Lychee Thandai

Ingredients
Lychee juice **125 ml**
Pineapple juice **125 ml**
Basil leaves **20 sprigs**
Coconut milk **60 ml**

Method
Blend all the ingredients well and pour into a glass.

Garnish Pineapple slice
Glass Goblet

Cucumber Surprise

Ingredients

Cucumber, dices into small pieces **7-8**

Rock salt **1 tbsp**

Cranberry juice **250 ml**

Method

Blend all the ingredients well and pour into a glass.

Garnish Diced cucumber

Glass Martini

Lemony Crimson

Ingredients

Grape juice **60 ml**
Cranberry juice **60 ml**
Orange juice **60 ml**
Lemon juice **10 ml**
Ginger ale to top up
Ice cubes

Method

Shake all the ingredients except ginger ale with ice and pour into a glass. Top up with ginger ale.

Garnish Orange and lemon spirals
Glass Tom Collins

Raspberry Virgin Daiquiri

Ingredients

Raspberry purée **1½ tbsp**
Lime juice, fresh **10 ml**
Sprite to top up

Method

Put all the ingredients in a glass and top up with Sprite.

Garnish Sugar coated lemon slice
Glass Martini

Sweet Virgin Mojito

Ingredients

Mint, fresh **8-10 leaves**
Sugar syrup **10 ml**
Lime juice **10 ml**
Crushed ice **½ glass**
Apple juice **60 ml**
Ice cubes

Method

Put all the ingredients together with ice and mix well.

Garnish Apple peel and mint leaves
Glass Tall glass

Monkey's Lunch

Ingredients
Mint **8-10 leaves**
Sugar syrup **10 ml**
Lemon juice **15 ml**

Method
Blend all the ingredients with crushed ice.

Garnish Mint leaves
Glass Old-fashioned

Olive Beach Island

Ingredients
Orange **3 wedges**
Watermelon **50 gm**
Ice **10-12 cubes**
Lime juice, fresh **30 ml**
Lemonade **200 ml**
Ice cubes

Method
Muddle orange wedges in a glass. Add mashed watermelon. Fill the glass with ice cubes and squeeze the lime juice. Top up with lemonade.

Garnish Watermelon
Glass Tall

Mango Melt

Ingredients
Mango, large, ripe ½
Vanilla ice-cream **1 scoop**
Cinnamon, ground **1 flat tbsp**
Ice cubes

Method
Put all the ingredients in a blender. Add ice and blend. Pour into a glass.

Garnish Cinnamon-dusted orange slice
Glass Cocktail

Shopping Gals

Ingredients

Tamarind purée **20 ml**

Lemons **2**

7up to top up

Ice cubes

Method

Put the ice cubes and all the ingredients in a shaker. Shake well and strain into a chilled glass.

Garnish Cherry and lemon spiral

Glass Martini

Ice Tea Raspberry

Ingredient
Raspberry purée **45 ml**
Tea **4 gm**
Water **120 ml**
Ice cubes

Method
Put raspberry purée in Tom Collins glass. Add ice and mix well. Top up with tea decoction.

Garnish Mint sprig
Glass Tom Collins

Tropical Treat

Ingredients

Pineapple juice **150 ml**
Coconut milk **30 ml**
Chocolate syrup **30 ml**
Ice cubes

Method

Blend all the ingredients with ice and pour into a glass.

Garnish Pineapple cone
Glass Tom Collins

Morning Dew

Ingredients

Green apple syrup **15 ml**
Green mint syrup **10 ml**
Lime juice **10 ml**
Sprite to top up
Ice cubes

Method

Put the apple syrup, mint syrup, and lime juice in a glass. Add ice cubes and top up with Sprite.

Garnish Mint sprig
Glass Pilsner

For A Makeover!

Ingredients
Mixed fruit juice **15 ml**
Grape juice **20 ml**
Apple syrup **15 ml**
Peach syrup **10 ml**
Ice cubes

Method
Shake all the ingredients with ice in a shaker and serve.

Glass Cooler

Jamaican Blast

Ingredients

Espresso **30 ml**

Vanilla ice-cream **1 scoop**

Vanilla essence **2 drops**

Coke to top up

Ice cubes

Method

Put espresso, vanilla ice-cream and essence in a blender and blend. Pour the mixture into a glass, add ice and top up with Coke.

Glass Pilsner

Orange Breeze

Ingredients

Orange **10 chunks**
Coriander leaf **1 sprig**
Orange juice, fresh **60 ml**
Lime juice **10 ml**
Sprite to top up
Crushed ice

Method

Muddle orange chunks and coriander leaves in a glass. Add lime and orange juice. Put crushed ice and top up with Sprite.

Garnish Orange wheel and coriander leaves
Glass Tom Collins

Summer King

Ingredients

Lime **1 wedge**
Mango purée **15 ml**
White grape juice **90 ml**
Sugar to rim the glass
Ice cubes

Method

Moisten the rim of a martini glass with the wedge of lime. Dip the rim into granulated sugar. Shake mango purée and grape juice with ice in a Boston shaker. Strain into the rimmed glass.

Garnish Sugar
Glass Martini

New Zealander

Ingredients

Kiwi, fresh **5 chunks**
Mint **6 leaves**
Lemon **3 chunks**
7up to top up
Ice cubes

Method

Muddle kiwi, mint, and lemon in a glass. Fill the glass with ice and top up with 7up. Stir slightly.

Garnish Lemon slice
Glass Tom Collins

Lychee Exotica

Ingredients
Lychee juice **150 ml**
Plain yoghurt **4 tbsp**
Banana, fresh **1**
Honey **15 ml**
Grenadine syrup **5 ml**
Ice cubes

Method
Put all the ingredients in a blender and blend with ice.

Garnish Banana slice
Glass Old-fashioned

Kiss Me Red!

Ingredients

Pineapple juice **30 ml**
Grape juice **60 ml**
Orange juice **60 ml**
Sugar syrup **5 ml**
Grenadine **10 ml**
7up to top up
Ice cubes

Method

Pour the juices over the ice in a glass and top up with 7up. Float grenadine on top and let it dribble through for effect.

Garnish Orange slice
Glass Tom Collins

Blue Hawaiian

Ingredients
Non-alcoholic blue curacao **30 ml**
Coconut cream **10 ml**
Pineapple juice **120 ml**
Ice cubes

Method
Shake all the ingredients with ice in a cocktail shaker. Strain into a glass filled with ice.

Garnish Pineapple flag
Glass Hurricane

Sunny Afternoon

Ingredients
Mango juice, fresh **90 ml**
Mint, fresh **6 leaves**
Lemon juice **5 ml**
Gomme syrup **10 ml**
Ice cubes

Method
Blend all the ingredients with ice and pour into a glass.

Garnish Mint sprig
Glass Margarita

Prince Charming

Ingredients

Pineapple juice **60 ml**
Orange juice **60 ml**
Lime juice **15 ml**
Grenadine **10 ml**
Club soda **1**
Ice cubes

Method

Put all the ingredients except the soda with ice in a shaker. Shake well and strain into a tall glass filled with ice. Top up with soda.

Garnish Orange slice
Glass Pilsner

Mint Loves Ginger

Ingredients

Mint, fresh **10-15 sprigs**
Ginger **5 gm**
Lime juice **60 ml**
Lime cordial **30 ml**
Lychee crush **30 ml**
Sugar syrup **30 ml**
Crushed ice

Method

Blend all the ingredients together. Pour into a glass.

Garnish Lime twist and mint sprig
Glass Imperial glass

Berry Sweetheart

Ingredients

Cranberry juice **90 ml**
Apple juice **90 ml**
Honey **30 ml**
Cherry **1**
Ice cubes

Method

Put ice in a glass and add all the ingredients except cherry. Stir and serve.

Garnish Cherry
Glass Highball

Kiwi Slush

Ingredients
Kiwi, fresh **2**
Lime juice **60 ml**
Kiwi syrup **45 ml**
Crushed ice **200 gm**

Method
Blend all the ingredients (except the kiwi) together. Pour the frozen slush into a glass. Add the minced chopped kiwi on top of the slush.

Garnish Kiwi slice
Glass Margarita

Mint Collins

Ingredients

Ginger juice **15 ml**
Mint **6 leaves**
Lemon juice **15 ml**
Fresh orange juice **120 ml**
Ice cubes

Method

Muddle mint with ginger juice. Add lemon juice and fresh orange juice with ice and shake well before pouring into a glass.

Garnish Orange quarters
Glass Tom Collins
Tip In case the guest does not like ginger juice you can use ginger ale instead.

Orange Dew

Ingredients

Cranberry juice **100 ml**
Orange syrup **10 ml**
Grenadine syrup **a dash**
Sugar syrup **15 ml**
Lemon juice **5 ml**
Orange zest
Ice cubes

Method

Shake all the ingredients well in a cocktail shaker with a few ice cubes and strain into a glass. Grate the orange zest on top.

Garnish Orange peel
Glass Martini

Virgin Sangria

Ingredients

Fruit mixer (chopped apple, orange, pineapple, kiwi, green olive, olive brine, passion fruit monin), fresh **3 tbsp**
Grape juice **150 ml**
Ice **4-6 cubes**
Watermelon slices

Method

Take fresh fruit mixer and keep in the refrigerator for 1 full day. Add the grape juice to 3 tbsp of fresh fruit mixer and 3-4 ice cubes.

Garnish Pineapple and watermelon
Glass Wine

Viola and Jane

Ingredients

Pineapple juice **120 ml**
Chocolate syrup **45 ml**
Coconut syrup **15 ml**
Ice cubes

Method

Shake all the ingredients with ice in a shaker and strain into a glass.

Garnish Chocolate cigar
Glass Tom Collins

Lusty Lemonade

Ingredients
Orange juice **100 ml**
Pineapple juice **100 ml**
Lemonade to top up
Ice cubes

Method
Pour orange and pineapple juice in a glass full of ice. Stir the mixture and top up with lemonade.

Garnish Orange slice and cherry
Glass Martini

Mango Sin

Ingredients

Mango juice **290 ml**

Mint and Basil leaves **10 sprigs each**

Method

Blend all the ingredients well. Pour into a glass.

Garnish Mint sprig and lime slice

Glass Beer pilsner

Herbal Lemonade

Ingredients

Mint **6-8 leaves**
Lemon **6-8 chunks**
Black pepper powder **a pinch**
Roasted cumin powder **a pinch**
Ginger ale **15 ml**
Honey **15 ml**
Angostura bitter **2-3 drops**
Lemonade to top up
Ice cubes

Method

Muddle all the ingredients and pour into a tall glass with ice. Top up with lemonade.

Garnish Mint leaves and cherry
Glass Tom Collins

Virgin Banana Daiquiri

Ingredients

Banana **½**
Milk **50 ml**
Cream **50 ml**
Sugar syrup **1 tsp**
Grenadine **10 ml**
Pomegranate seeds for garnish
Ice cubes

Method

Blend banana, milk, cream, and sugar syrup with ice in a blender. Pour grenadine gently with an inverted spoon and serve chilled.

Garnish Pomegranate seeds
Glass Hurricane

Caribbean Delight

Ingredients

Pineapple juice **60 ml**
Mango juice **60 ml**
Orange juice **60 ml**
Coconut cream **20 ml**
Mint sprig for garnish
Ice cubes

Method

Mix all the juices together in a tall glass with lots of ice and float coconut cream on top.

Garnish Mint sprig
Glass Tall

Sun Downer

Ingredients

White grape juice **60 ml**
Cold sparkling water **40 ml**
Fresh mint sprig for garnish
Ice cubes

Method

Pour all the ingredients into a pilsner glass with ice. Stir and serve chilled.

Garnish Mint sprig
Glass Pilsner

Peach Julius

Ingredients
Ginger **4 chunks**
Lime **5 chunks**
Mint **4 leaves**
Peach and apricot crush **45 ml**
Crushed ice

Method
In a shaker, add all the ingredients, muddle well and pour into a goblet. Add crushed ice and serve.

Garnish Apricot slice
Glass Goblet

Malta Mojito

Ingredients

Malta, fresh **4-5 cubes**
Demerara sugar **1 tsp**
Mint, fresh **8 leaves**
Lime wedges **3 pieces**
Crushed ice **1 scoop**
7up / Sprite to top up

Method

Pour demerara sugar into a glass and muddle. Add mint leaves, malta, and lime wedges; muddle together. Top up with crushed ice and 7up / Sprite.

Garnish Malta slice and mint leaves
Glass Old-fashioned

Basil-ica

Ingredients

Basil **3 leaves**

Lychee juice **45 ml**

Ice cubes

Method

In a shaker, put all the ingredients. Add ice cubes and shake vigorously, pour into a tango glass.

Garnish A basil leaf and a twisted lemon peel

Glass Tango

Raspberry Lyrics

Ingredients
Raspberry purée **45 ml**
Lime juice **10 ml**
Sugar syrup **10 ml**
Soda / 7up **Half bottle**
Crushed ice

Method
Pour all the ingredients into a cocktail shaker. Shake well and serve.

Garnish Lime slice
Glass Brandy balloon

Peach Loves Ginger

Ingredients
Peach purée **30 ml**
Peach half **1 piece**
Ginger ale **100 ml**
Crushed ice

Method
Put half of a peach and crushed ice in a blender and blend for a minute. Pour peach purée and the blended peach into a cocktail shaker. Shake well and serve.

Garnish Mint sprig
Glass Tall

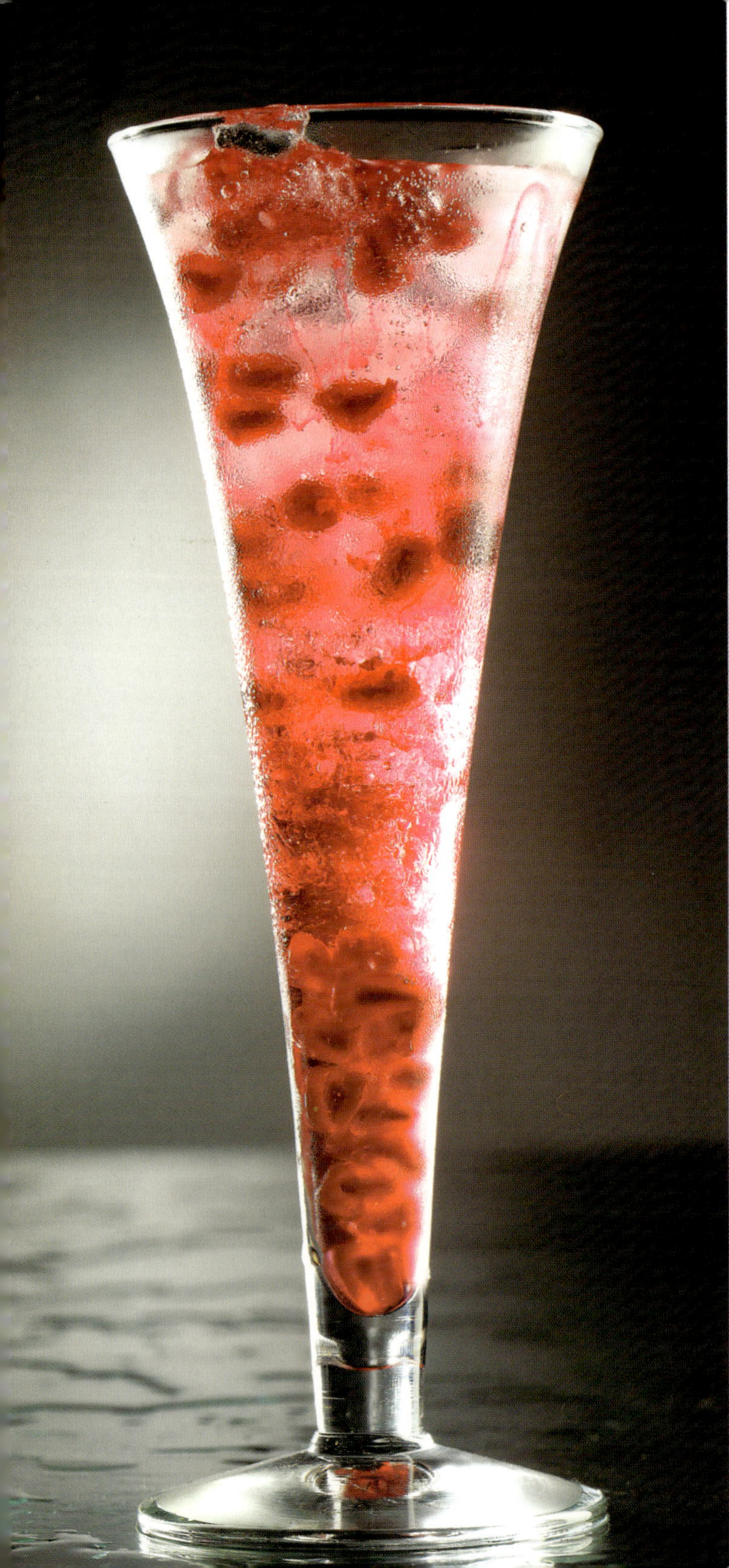

Shirley Temple

Ingredients

Grenadine syrup **15 ml**
Lemon juice **10 ml**
Pomegranate seeds **12-14 seeds**
7up to top up
Ice cubes

Method

Pour 7up in a tall glass over ice, add lemon juice and grenadine syrup.

Garnish Pomegranate seeds
Glass Tall

Jolly Roger's Special

Ingredients

Lychees, deseeded **10 pieces**
Coconuts, tender **2**
Whipped cream **1 tbsp**
Water sugar, if required, chilled **300 ml**
Ice cubes

Method

Break open the coconuts. Strain the coconut water and keep aside. Scrape out the inner tender layers of coconut. Make sure its soft, thin and tender. Now add this to a blender along with lychees, whipped cream and sugar. Whirl until it forms a smooth paste. Add coconut water, chilled water and blend again till frothy. Add ice cubes and serve.

Garnish Lychee
Glass Zombie

Afternoon Punch

Ingredients

Watermelon **few chunks**
Kiwi, fresh, cut into pieces **1**
Pomegranate, fresh, peeled **1**
Mango, fresh, cut **1**
Pineapple **few chunks**
Lime juice, fresh **10 ml**
Pomegranate seeds for garnish
Ice cubes

Method

Take a blender, add ice cubes and freshly cut fruits into it. Pour in the lime juice and blend till it becomes a smoothie and serve.

Garnish Pomegranate seeds
Glass Margarita

Lady in Pink

Ingredients
Pineapple juice **90 ml**
Orange juice **90 ml**
Strawberry crush **30 ml**
Peach compote **2**
Crushed ice

Method
Blend all the ingredients with crushed ice. Pour into a glass.

Garnish Pineapple or orange slice
Glass Pilsner

Cool Mango Delight

Ingredients
Canned mango juice **60 ml**
Coke **a splash**
Mango, fresh, sliced for garnish
Ice cubes

Method
Take a beer mug and fill it up with ice. Add mango juice. Pour the Coke gently, it should not mix with the mango juice. Serve.

Garnish Mango or lemon slice
Glass Beer mug

Summer Melon

Ingredients

Watermelon juice **100 ml**
Watermelon syrup **15 ml**
Lemon **2 wedges**
Basil **3 leaves**
Ginger ale **120 ml**
Ice cubes

Method

Muddle together lemon wedges and basil leaves in a cocktail shaker. Add all the ingredients except ginger ale with ice cubes. Shake well and strain into a tall glass. Top with ginger ale.

Garnish Watermelon slice
Glass Tall pilsner

Cucumber Anise

Ingredients

De-seeded cucumber juice **150 ml (No skin)**
Anise syrup **15 ml**
Lime juice **5 ml**
Coriander **3 sprigs**
Ice cubes

Method

Pour all the ingredients into a shaker with ice and shake well. Pour and serve.

Garnish Coriander sprig and star anise
Glass Highball

Miami Beach

Ingredients
Tomato juice **120 ml**
Mint **4-5**
Tabasco **4 drops**
Worcestershire sauce **4 drops**
Lime juice **5 ml**
Salt **a pinch**
Pepper **a pinch**

For the salt rim
Lemon wedge **1**
Salt **100 gm**
Ice cubes

Method
Pour all the ingredients into a blender with ice. Blend well and serve in a salt-rimmed glass.

Garnish Salt-rimmed (only half rim) and lemon wedge
Glass Margarita

Aqua Blue

Ingredients

Apple juice **125 ml**
Blue Curacao syrup **10 ml**
Peach syrup **15 ml**
Lemon juice **15 ml**
Ice cubes

Method

Shake all the ingredients in a cocktail shaker and pour into a large rock glass filled with ice.

Garnish Apple slices
Glass Rock

Virgin Blue Deliti

Ingredients

Blueberry purée **1½ tbsp**
Lime juice **10 ml**
Apple juice **60 ml**

Method

Mix all the ingredients well and pour into a glass.

Garnish Apple slice
Glass Martini

Midnight Queen
(Creamy Coffee)

Ingredients

Coffee **30 ml**
Milk **100 ml**
Cocoa **30 ml**
Hazelnut syrup **15 ml**
Cream **30 ml**

Method

Shake coffee, milk, cocoa, and hazelnut syrup and pour into a glass.

Garnish Cream and coffee beans
Glass Highball

Sangria Blast

Ingredients

Red grape juice **90 ml**
Pomegranate juice **60 ml**
Lemon wedge **1**
Rosemary **a sprig**
Green apple, chopped **2 tbsp**
Pomegranate seeds **1 tbsp**
Ice cubes

Method

Muddle the rosemary and lemon wedge in a cocktail shaker, add the juices and stir with ice cubes. Strain into a wine glass and serve with chopped apples and pomegranate seeds.

Garnish Apple cubes and pomegranate seeds
Glass Wine

Kolkata Cooler

Ingredients

Gondhoraj lemon **1**
Kiwi syrup **45 ml**
Lychee juice **45 ml**
Rock salt **to taste**
Lemon juice **5 ml**
Ice cubes

Method

Bruise the gondhoraj lemon with kiwi syrup and strain; add the lychee juice, rock salt and lemon juice. Blend with ice. Serve as a frappe.

Garnish Kiwi slice
Glass Martini

Raspberry Ice Tea

Ingredients

Raspberry syrup **60 ml**
Lemon juice **5 ml**
Raspberry, whole **3**
Sugar syrup **10 ml**
Tea concoction **120 ml**
Mint sprigs **a few**
Lemon wheels **4**
Ice cubes

Method

Take the Napoli grande glass, fill it with ice. Pour lemon juice, raspberry syrup, and hint of sugar syrup. Float raspberries and top up with tea concoction.

Garnish Lemon wheel
Glass Napoli grande

Tibetan Road

Ingredients

Apple syrup **10 ml**
Aloe vera and
apple juice **120 ml**
Coriander **3 leaves**
Mandarin (Indian orange) **½**
Ice cubes

Method

In a mixing glass, muddle Mandarin and coriander. Add apple juice and syrup, shake and double strain into a glass filled with ice.

Garnish Coriander stalk
Glass Tom Collins

Orange Valley

Ingredients

Sweet lime, quartered **1**
Orange juice **90 ml**
Green tea concoction **120 ml**
Sugar syrup **15 ml**
Lemon juice **10 ml**
Ice cubes

Method

Bruise the sweet lime quarters with lemon juice and sugar syrup. Mix well with fresh orange juice. Pour into the glass, loaded with ice and top up with green tea concoction.

Garnish Mint sprigs and sweet lime wheel
Glass Napoli grande

Eden's Mojo

Ingredients

Mint **12 leaves**
Caramel sauce **20 ml**
Lime juice **30 ml**
Cherry for garnish
Ice cubes

Method

Mix all the ingredients in a glass, stir and serve.

Garnish Cherry
Glass Cocktail

Apple Fizz

Ingredient

Apple syrup **5 ml**
Brown sugar **1 sachet**
Apple, chopped into chunks **¼ apple**
Apple juice **100 ml**
Ginger ale **30 ml**
Ice cubes

Method

Put apple syrup, brown sugar, apple chunks, and apple juice in the blender. Add ice and blend for a while. Pour the mixture into a glass and top up with ginger ale.

Garnish Apple slice
Glass Martini

Peppercorn Flip

Ingredients

Peppercorns **4**
Lime **5 wedges**
Tender coconut **1**
Cherries for garnish

Method

Muddle peppercorns and lime wedges in a glass. Top up with coconut water and stir.

Garnish Cherries
Glass Highball

Dynamite Milkshake

Ingredient

Pineapple **20 gm**
Apple **20 gm**
Orange **20 gm**
Peach purée **30 ml**
Milk **150 ml**
Orange juice **60 ml**
Pineapple juice **60 ml**
Apple juice **60 ml**
Vanilla
ice-cream **1 scoop**

Method

Place the chunks of pineapple, apple, and orange in the base of the glass. Add a measure of monin peach purée. Top up with blended milk shake. To make milk shake, mix orange, pineapple, and apple juice in milk and shake or blend well. Add vanilla ice-cream just before serving.

Garnish Chopped pineapple, apple, and orange
Glass Tall

Star Anise Flirt

Ingredients
Mango nectar **150 ml**
Cranberry juice **150 ml**
Lime juice **just a dash**
Star anise **1**

Method
Add all the ingredients except star anise. Stir well and serve.

Garnish Star anise
Glass Goblet

Lone Ranger

Ingredients
Apple juice **300 ml**
Coconut cream **20 ml**
Strawberries **4**
Ice cubes

Method
Blend all the ingredients with ice and strain into a glass.

Garnish Apple slice
Glass Pilsner

Burning Kiss

Ingredients
Orange juice **120 ml**
Pineapple juice **120 ml**
Lime juice **5 ml**
Rose syrup **a dash**

Method
Mix all the ingredients. Stir well and serve.

Garnish Slit chilli
Glass Pilsner

Smooth Deception

Ingredients

Orange juice **80 ml**
Pineapple juice **80 ml**
Apple juice **80 ml**
Watermelon juice **80 ml**
Banana **1**
Ice cubes

Method

Blend all the ingredients and ice together; pour into a glass.

Garnish Apple slices
Glass Pilsner

Kiwi Sunshine

Ingredients

Kiwi purée **60 ml**
Sprite **120 ml**
Sweet lime froth **3 tbsp**
Kiwi chunks **2 tbsp**
Crushed ice

Method

Blend the kiwi in a blender and pour over crushed ice in a glass. Add Sprite on top. Blend the sweet lime juice in a blender to make froth. Pour the froth over the glass and sprinkle kiwi chunks on top.

Garnish Kiwi slice
Glass Tom Collins

Walk Me Down

Ingredients
Orange juice **120 ml**
Strawberry crush **60 ml**
Soda **60 ml**
Crushed ice

Method
Pour the strawberry crush on crushed ice in a glass. Add orange juice on top, followed with soda.

Garnish Lime wedge
Glass Tulip

Chamomile Love

Ingredients

Lemon leaves **3 pieces**
Dried chamomile **¼ tsp**
Wildflower honey cooler
Ice cubes

Method

In a small pot, bring a cup of water to a boil over high heat. Remove the pot from the heat. Stir in the dried chamomile and lemon leaves. Cover and steep for 10 minutes. Meanwhile, place a large strainer lined with cheesecloth over another pot or heatproof bowl. Strain the tea, pressing on the chamomile and lemon leaves to extract all liquid. Stir in organic wild flower honey until it dissolves, and let the mix cool completely. Fill a tall glass with ice. Pour the liquid over ice and garnish with lemon spiral.

Garnish Lemon spiral
Glass Tall

Glowing Sunset

Ingredients

Orange **4-5 chunks**
Lemon **4-5 chunks**
Orange juice **200 ml**
Grenadine **15 ml**
Crushed ice

Method

Muddle orange and lemon chunks in a cocktail shaker. Add crushed ice and stir . Pour the mixture into a glass. Add orange juice and grenadine on top.

Garnish Orange spiral
Glass Pilsner

Cherry Basil Cooler

Ingredients

Cherries, fresh **7-8 pieces**
Basil **7-8 leaves**
Lemon juice **15 ml**
Lemonade to top up
Crushed ice

Method

Muddle fresh cherries and basil leaves in a cocktail shaker. Add lemon juice and crushed ice. Stir and pour the mixture in a glass and top up with lemonade.

Garnish Cherry
Glass Hurricane

Baby Love

Ingredients

Coconut milk **30 ml**
Pineapple juice **60 ml**
Banana syrup **30 ml**
Banana **1**
Cream **30 ml**
Ice cubes

Method

Blend all the ingredients together including cream and pour over ice. Serve chilled.

Garnish Banana slice
Glass Brandy balloon

Mango Raspberry Frappe

Ingredients

Mango purée **60 ml**
Raspberry purée **60 ml**
Lime juice **10 ml**
Sprite to top up
Crushed ice

Method

Pour mango, raspberry purées and lime juice in a glass filled with crushed ice. Top up with Sprite and serve.

Garnish Mint sprig
Glass Hurricane

Strawberry Lyrics

Ingredients

Strawberries **4 pieces**
Lemon **6 chunks**
Strawberry crush **30 ml**
Ginger ale to top up
Crushed ice

Method

Muddle lemon chunks with strawberry crush. Fill the glass with crushed ice and top up with ginger ale.

Garnish Lemon slices
Glass Roly poly

Apple Cinnamon Virgin Mojito

Ingredients

Red apple chunks **½ apple**
Mint, fresh **10-12 leaves**
Cinnamon syrup **10 ml**
Cinnamon stick **1**
Apple juice to top up
Crushed ice

Method

Muddle red apple chunks, mint leaves, and monin cinnamon syrup in a glass filled with crushed ice. Top up with apple juice.

Garnish Cinnamon stick
Glass Tom Collins

Cranberry Rooibos Iced Tea

Ingredients

Cranberry juice **40 ml**
Sugar syrup **15 ml**
Rooibos Tea* **1 cup**
Ice cubes

Method

Pour the cranberry juice and sugar syrup into a tall ice filled glass. Add tea and serve.

Garnish Any fresh fruit slice
Glass Tom Collins

*Rooibos is a plant and is used in making Rooibos Tea

Awesome Foursome

Ingredients

Orange juice **120 ml**
Pineapple juice **20 ml**
Almond syrup **10 ml**
Cherry syrup **5 ml**
Ice cubes

Method

Put all the ingredients in the cocktail shaker; shake and pour into a glass over ice.

Garnish Pineapple slice and orange spiral
Glass Hurricane

Passion Fruit Cooler

Ingredients

Passion fruit purée **20 ml**
Orange juice **60 ml**
Pineapple juice **60 ml**
Sprite to top up

Method

Shake the juices with ice and purée and pour into a tall glass. Top up with Sprite and serve.

Garnish Orange or pineapple wedge
Glass Cocktail

Moulin Rouge

Ingredients

Cranberry juice **180 ml**
Ginger syrup **10 ml**
Vanilla ice-cream **1 scoop**

Method

Put all the ingredients into a cocktail shaker; shake well and pour into a glass.

Garnish Ginger juliennes
Glass Hurricane

Watermelon Lyrics

Ingredients

Watermelon, fresh **5-6 chunks**
Mint, fresh **4-5 leaves**
Lemon **3 chunks**
Demerara sugar **1 tsp**
Crushed ice

Method

Muddle all the ingredients in a glass. Add crushed ice and top up with lemonade.

Garnish Watermelon slice
Glass Old-fashioned

Mint Zing

Ingredients
Cucumber **4**
Green apple syrup **10 ml**
Apple juice **60 ml**
Mint **8-10 leaves**
Red bull to top up
Crushed ice

Method
Blend all the ingredients in the blender without red bull. Pour into a glass and top up with red bull.

Garnish Mint sprig
Glass Hurricane

Berry Patch

Ingredients
Blueberry **2 bar spoons**
Strawberry purée **30 ml**
Vanilla ice-cream **2 scoops**
Crushed ice

Method
Put all the ingredients into a blender; blend and pour into a glass.

Garnish Blueberry purée
Glass Pilsner

Apple Soaked Mojito

Ingredients

Apple, fresh **5-6 chunks**
Mint, fresh **4-5 leaves**
Lemon **3 chunks**
Demerara sugar **1 tsp**
Lemonade or Sprite to top up
Crushed ice

Method

Muddle all the ingredients in a glass. Add crushed ice and top up with lemonade.

Garnish Mint sprig
Glass Old-fashioned

Coy

Ingredients

Pineapple juice **50 ml**
Mango juice **50 ml**
Orange juice **50 ml**

Method

Shake all the ingredients in a shaker. Pour into the glass.

Garnish Pineapple half wheel / coconut cream
Glass Pilsner

Tropical Cruises

Ingredients
Apple, fresh **2 chunks**
Pineapple, fresh **2 chunks**
Papaya, fresh **2 chunks**
Apple juice **30 ml**
Crushed ice

Method
Blend all the ingredients in a blender and serve.

Garnish Papaya slice
Glass Margarita

Orange Mint Tea

Ingredients

Orange juice **4 cups**
Water **2 cups**
Black tea powder /
Tea bags **2**
Mint **10-12 leaves**
Sugar **2 tbsp**

Method

Boil water and add tea, mint, and sugar. Strain. Then mix the orange juice and chill before serving.

Garnish Mint sprig
Glass Tom collins

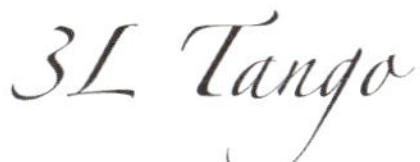

3L Tango

Ingredients

Lychee crush **30 ml**
Lime juice **30 ml**
Lemonade to top up

Method

Shake all the ingredients in a shaker. Pour into a glass.

Garnish Lime wedge
Glass Pilsner

Plum Fantasy

Ingredients

Californian plum, fresh **5-6 chunks**
Lemon juice, fresh **5 ml**
Apple juice **60 ml**
Anise syrup **5 ml**
Crushed ice

Method

Blend all the ingredients in a blender and serve.

Garnish Plum
Glass Margarita

Berry Splash

Ingredients

Cranberry juice **50 ml**
Strawberry juice **50 ml**
Soda **a splash**
Cherry for garnish
Crushed ice

Method

Shake all the ingredients in a shaker. Pour into a ice filled glass.

Garnish Cherry
Glass Pilsner

King Kong Bomb

Ingredients

Red bull **350 ml**
Cream **20 ml**
Sugar syrup **1 tsp**

Method

Serve the red bull in a highball glass only 3 quarters full. Pour a mixture of cream and sugar syrup into a shot glass and leave it to float. Do not use ice, but can use crushed ice, if required.

Garnish No Garnish. The float acts as a garnish.
Glass Highball and shot

Coffee Vanilla Bliss

Ingredients

Milk **150 ml**
Instant coffee **4 tbsp**
Vanilla ice-cream **60 gm**
Bananas, sliced, frozen **2**
Brown sugar **to taste**
Coffee beans for garnish

Method

Mix milk and coffee powder in the food processor. Add vanilla ice-cream, bananas and sugar to taste. Blend until smooth. Pour the mixture into the glass and serve.

Garnish Coffee beans
Glass Highball

Apple Grape Delight

Ingredients
Grapes **5 chunks**
Mint, large **5 leaves**
Hazelnut syrup **10 ml**
Apple juice to top up
Ice cubes

Method
Take a cocktail shaker, muddle grapes and mint leaves and shake well. Add ice, hazelnut syrup, and apple juice; shake once again. Then double strain and pour into a glass.

Glass Martini

Basil Blast

Ingredients
Orange **6 chunks**
Basil, large **2 leaves**
Mint, large **2 leaves**
Sugar **1 tsp**
Sprite to top up
Ice cubes

Method
Take a cocktail shaker, add orange, mint and sugar. Then gently muddle all the ingredients. Add ice cubes and shake. Top up with Sprite and serve.

Garnish Orange slice and basil leaves
Glass Tall

Mint Gypsy

Ingredients
Mint leaves **4-5 sprigs**
Peach and apricot crush **30 ml**
Sprite to top up
Crushed ice

Method
Put mint leaves in a tall glass and muddle. Pour peach and apricot crush. Fill ⅔rd of the glass with ice. Then fill the rest of the glass with club soda and stir again.

Garnish Mint leaves
Glass Highball

Olive Special

Ingredients

Grape juice **120 ml**
Olives **5-6 seedless pieces**
Lemon juice, fresh **5 ml**
Club soda to top up
Ice cubes

Method

Pour grape juice into a shaker. Muddle olives in the grape juice to extract flavour. Fill a beer glass with lots of ice cubes. Pour muddled ingredients into the glass and add lime juice. Top up with club soda.

Garnish Seedless olives on a stick
Glass Beer mug

Breakfast Delight

Ingredients

Banana **1**
Yoghurt **60 gm**
Orange juice **50 ml**
Strawberry, fresh **5-6**
Pineapple, peeled **2-3 slices**
Cherry for garnish

Method

Blend all the ingredients to a smooth purée and pour into a tall glass.

Garnish Cherry
Glass Tall

Lemon Sunrise

Ingredients

Mint **5-10 leaves**
Cucumber, diced **2 tbsp**
Lemon juice **5 ml**
Ginger ale to top up
Rock salt for garnish
Ice cubes

Method

Take cucumber and mint leaves in a cocktail shaker. Add lemon juice. Muddle all the ingredients together with ice cubes. Pour and serve.

Garnish Cucumber slices and rock salt
Glass Tom Collins

Organic Kokum Mango Delight

Ingredients
Organic kokum juice **30 ml**
Mango juice **180 ml**
Lemon **1**
Crushed ice

Method
In a cocktail shaker, add organic kokum juice, mango juice and a freshly squeezed lemon. Shake well with crushed ice and pour into a glass rimmed with fine sugar.

Garnish Mango slices
Glass Old-fashioned

Variation To enjoy a frozen kokum margarita, blend 8-10 cubes of ice, 30 ml of kokum juice, 60 ml of tequila and 15 ml of freshly squeezed lemon juice to form a thick slush. Serve in a salt-rimmed large margarita glass.

Vampire Kiss

Ingredients

Green tea, cold **100 ml**
Sprite **100 ml**
Blue curacao **30 ml**
Mint purée, fresh **30 ml**
Crushed ice

Method

Take a tall glass and fill it with ice. Pour blue curacao and mint purée. Add Sprite and green tea.

Garnish Cherry
Glass Tall

Mango Knock Out

Ingredients

Mango juice, fresh **120 ml**
Yoghurt **2 tbsp**
Lemon juice, fresh **5 ml**
Green chillies **1-2**

Method

Mix mango juice and fresh yoghurt in a glass. Add one green chilli and a dash of lemon juice. Blend all the ingredients together. Pour into a glass.

Garnish Green chilli
Glass Martini

Dates Surprise

Ingredients
Dates **30 gm**
Dry dates **30 gm**
Vanilla ice-cream **1 scoop**
Banana **1 small**
Vanilla essence **1 tsp**
Crushed ice

Method
Soak dates and dry dates in hot water for an hour. De-seed and blend the pulp with all the other ingredients along with crushed ice.

Garnish Date, de-seeded
Glass Tall

Melon Cooler

Ingredients
Pineapple juice **60 ml**
Orange juice **60 ml**
Watermelon syrup **15 ml**
7up to top up
Ice cubes

Method
Shake all the ingredients together and strain into a glass over ice cubes. Top up with 7up.

Garnish Watermelon slice
Glass Tom Collins

Guava Punch

Ingredients
Guava juice **120 ml**
Lemon juice **10 ml**
Tabasco **a dash**
Black salt **a pinch**
Coriander **5 leaves**

Method
Blend together all the ingredients with ice.

Garnish Guava slice
Glass Old-fashioned

Merry Christmas

Ingredients

Mint leaves, fresh **a few**
Sugar syrup **½ tsp**
Orange juice **120 ml**
Lemon juice **½ tsp**
Pomegranate juice **150 ml**
Mint syrup **½ tsp**
Orange **a slice**
Ice cubes

Method

In a goblet add some crushed ice along with fresh mint leaves, sugar syrup, fresh orange and lemon juice. Muddle the ingredients together. Add the remaining ingredients and serve.

Garnish Orange wheel
Glass Goblet

Ingredients

Pineapple juice **150 ml**
Lychee crush **30 ml**
Lychee juice **50 ml**
Vanilla ice cream **2 scoops**
Pineapple and cherry, fresh for garnish

Method

Blend pineapple juice, lychee crush, lychee juice, and one scoop of vanilla ice-cream in a blender. Pour into a glass. Top with remaining vanilla ice-cream scoop. Serve immediately.

Garnish Pineapple slice and cherry
Glass Tall

Fanta Grape Ecstasy

Ingredients

Red grape juice **90 ml**
Lychee juice **120 ml**
Orange juice **90 ml**
Fanta **30 ml**

Method

Add the red grape juice at the bottom of the tall glass. Top up with lychee and orange juice. With the help of a bar spoon. Float Fanta on top and serve chilled.

Garnish Lychee slice
Glass Highball

Ice Tea Canvas

Ingredients

Mint tea concoction **120 ml**
Sugar syrup **20 ml**
Lemon juice **20 ml**
Grenadine syrup **a dash**
Crushed ice

Method

In a glass half-filled with crushed ice, pour lemon juice, sugar syrup, little mint tea, and then slide a dash of grenadine syrup. Add some more ice and top up with mint tea.

Garnish Lemon wheels
Glass Pilsner

The Chuski

Ingredients

Mint syrup **20 ml**
Orange crush **20 ml**
Pomegranate syrup **20 ml**
Strawberry crush **20 ml**
Lemon slice for garnish
Crushed ice

Method

Fill three fourths of the glass with crushed ice, add orange crush, strawberry crush, and pomegranate syrup. Top the glass with crushed ice and add the mint syrup and lemon slice.

Garnish Lemon slice
Glass Short pilsner

Appletini

Ingredients
Apple juice **90 ml**
Lemon juice **10 ml**
Sprite **30 ml**
Lemon spiral for garnish
Apple slices for garnish
Ice cubes

Method
Put some lemon juice and chilled apple juice in the glass. Add little ice and top up with Sprite.

Garnish Apple slice
Glass Martini

Crocodile Cooler

Ingredients

Cucumber juice **120 ml**
Mint leaves **a few sprigs**
Honey **20 ml**
Lemon juice **10 ml**
Salt **¼ tsp**
Cucumber crocodile for garnish
Crushed ice

Method

Blend all the ingredients with crushed ice. Pour and serve.

Garnish Crocodile cucumber stick
Glass Old-fashioned

Orange Loves Pineapple

Ingredients

Pineapple juice **60 ml**
Orange juice **60 ml**
Vanilla ice-cream **60 ml**
Pineapple slice for garnish
Crushed ice

Method

Blend orange juice, pineapple juice, and a scoop of vanilla ice-cream. Pour into a glass and top up with some crushed ice.

Garnish Pineapple slice
Glass Hurricane

Strawberry and Orange Bliss

Ingredients

Strawberry purée **30 ml**
Lemon juice **5 ml**
Sugar syrup **5 ml**
Orange juice **100 ml**
Ginger ale **100 ml**
Ice cubes

Method

Pour all the ingredients in a cocktail shaker with ice cubes. Shake well and serve.

Garnish A mint sprig
Glass Goblet

Rose Lemonade

Ingredients
Lemon chunks **4-5 pieces**
Lemon juice **45 ml**
Sugar syrup **20 ml**
Rose syrup **15 ml**
Water **120 ml**
Ice cubes

Method
Put all the ingredients except water in a mixing glass. Muddle with 3 cubes of ice and pour into a beer pilsner with ice. Top up with water.

Garnish Lemon wheel
Glass Pilsner

Devil's Passion

Ingredients
Guava juice **90 ml**
Lemon juice **10 ml**
Mint syrup **5 ml**
Tabasco **a few drops**
Rock salt **a pinch**
Ice cubes

Method
Put all the ingredients in a shaker, fill it with ice and shake well.

Garnish Mint sprig
Glass Old-fashioned

Angel's Desire

Ingredients

Apple juice **60 ml**
Cranberry juice **60 ml**
Strawberry purée **15 ml**
Strawberry ice-cream **1 scoop**
Ice cubes

Method

Put all the ingredients in a cocktail shaker. Fill with ice and shake well.

Garnish Mint sprig
Glass Hurricane

Mint Sprite Sparkle

Ingredients

Peppermint syrup **5 ml**
Lemon juice **5 ml**
Sprite **120 ml**
Crushed ice

Method

Pour peppermint syrup with lemon juice on crushed ice in a tall glass. Top up with Sprite.

Garnish Mint sprig
Glass Tall

Ingredients
Lychee juice **160 ml**
Lemon juice **20 ml**
Khus syrup **60 ml**
Sugar syrup **20 ml**
Crushed ice

Method
Put all the ingredients in a blender with crushed ice and blend well.

Garnish Lychee
Glass Hurricane

Watermelon Lemonade

Ingredients
Watermelon juice **120 ml**
Lemon juice **5 ml**
Sugar syrup **5 ml**
Ice cubes

Method
Stir all the ingredients into a tall glass. Serve chilled.

Garnish Watermelon slice
Glass Tall

Innocent Passion

Ingredients

Passion fruit syrup **10 ml**
Lemon juice **10 ml**
Sprite **60 ml**
Cranberry juice **60 ml**
Crushed ice

Method

Put some ice in a glass, add passion fruit syrup, lemon juice, Sprite, and float cranberry juice on top.

Garnish Lemon slice
Glass Jazz

Hibiscus Sparkler

Ingredients

Mint **5 leaves**
Black grapes, seedless **6-8 pieces**
Sugar syrup **20 ml**
Cinnamon stick **1**
Apple juice **50 ml**
Hibiscus tea decoction **100 ml**
Sparkling water to top up
Crushed ice

Method

Put black grapes, mint leaves, sugar syrup, and cinnamon stick in the glass. Muddle properly. Add crushed ice, apple juice and hibiscus tea decoction, stir gently. Top with sparkling water and serve.

Garnish Black grape skewer
Glass Tom Collins

Surfers' Paradise

Ingredients

Khus syrup **10 ml**
Pineapple juice **90 ml**
Vanilla ice-cream **1 scoop**
Ice cubes

Method

Shake khus syrup and pineapple juice with ice and pour into a cocktail glass. Add a scoop of vanilla ice-cream on top.

Garnish Sliced almonds
Glass Cocktail

Orange Mint Virgin Mojito

Ingredients
Orange **3-4 chunks**
Mint **6-7 leaves**
Lemon **3 wedges**
Lime juice **10 ml**
Orange juice **90 ml**
Demerara sugar **1 bar spoon**
Crushed ice

Method

Squeeze lemon wedges into the glass. Muddle orange chunks, mint leaves, demerara sugar, and lime juice. Add crushed ice, disperse it within the glass. Add orange juice and a splash of soda.

Garnish Orange slices and mint sprigs
Glass Tom Collins

Hot Kiss

Ingredients
Vanilla ice-cream **1 scoop**
Strawberry syrup **5 ml**
Orange juice **90 ml**
Pineapple juice **90 ml**
Crushed ice

Method

Put all the ingredients in the blender and blend well. Pour and serve in a chilled glass.

Garnish Pineapple slice
Glass Hurricane

Tickly Plum

Ingredients

Plum, fresh **50 gm**
Apple juice **75 ml**
Peach syrup **20 ml**
Sparkling water to top up

Method

Blend fresh plum, apple juice, and peach syrup. Pour the mixture without straining in a chilled glass. Top with sparkling water.

Garnish Plum wheel
Glass Martini

Yellow Splash

Ingredients

Coriander leaves, fresh **1 sprig**
Mint leaves, fresh **2-3 sprigs**
Pineapple juice, fresh **200 ml**
Kiwi syrup **15 ml**

Method

In a glass muddle coriander and fresh mint leaves. Top with ice cubes. Add fresh pineapple juice and kiwi syrup, shake well. Pour the mix into a glass without ice.

Garnish Pineapple slice
Glass Highball

Ginger Sling

Ingredients
Lemon **6-7 chunks**
Mint **5-6 leaves**
White sugar **5 gm**
Lemon juice **15 ml**
Ginger syrup **30 ml**
Blue curacao **15 ml**
Lemonade to top up
Crushed ice

Method
Muddle lemon chunks, mint leaves, and white grain sugar. Pour lemon juice, ginger syrup, blue curaçao into a glass half filled with ice. Top up with lemonade and stir gently.

Glass Hurricane

Muesli and Apple Smoothie

Ingredients
Yoghurt **100 ml**
Dried apricots **30 gm**
Prunes **20 gm**
Muesli **40 gm**
Apple juice **50 ml**
Honey **20 ml**

Method
Blend yoghurt, dried apricots, prunes, muesli, and apple juice together. Pour into a glass.

Garnish Mint sprig
Glass Pilsner

Apricot Lemonade

Ingredients
Peach syrup **10 ml**
Apricot syrup **10 ml**
Lemon juice **10 ml**
Lemonade to top up
Ice cubes

Method
Add all the ingredients into a glass filled with ice.

Garnish Mint sprig
Glass Highball

Power Protein Smoothie

Ingredients
Yoghurt **100 ml**
Bananas **60 gm**
Oatmeal **25 gm**
Vanilla essence **5 ml**
Honey **30 ml**

Method
Mix yoghurt, bananas and oatmeal. Blend it well. Pour and serve.

Garnish Vanilla essence and honey
Glass Pilsner

Pretty Sweetheart

Ingredients
Watermelon, fresh **1 large cappuccino cup**
Celery, fresh **1 stick**
Pomegranate **1 small cup**
Ice cubes

Method

Put all the ingredients into the juicer. Mix well and serve in a chilled glass filled with ice cubes.

Garnish Watermelon slice and celery stick
Glass Pilsner

Mushy Melon

Ingredients
Watermelon syrup **15 ml**
Pineapple juice **45 ml**
Lemon juice **15 ml**
Ice cubes

Method
Pour the ingredients into a shaker with lots of ice cubes. Shake well. Pour into a glass.

Garnish Pineapple slice
Glass Frosted margarita

Hawaiian Dreams

Ingredients
Mango juice **40 ml**
Pineapple juice **40 ml**
Orange juice **40 ml**
Coconut cream **15 ml**
Green apple syrup **30 ml**

Method
Pour all the ingredients in the shaker with ice. Shake well and strain into a glass.

Garnish Sliced coconut
Glass Hurricane

Peanut Butter Shake

Ingredients
Peanut butter **4 full bar spoons**
Milk **150 ml**
Vanilla latte **60 ml**
Ice **4 cubes**

Method
Put all the ingredients into the blender and blend well. Pour and serve.

Garnish Peanuts
Glass Pilsner

Cool Sensation

Ingredients

Grenadine syrup **30 ml**
Apple juice **90 ml**
Sugar syrup **a dash**
Lemon juice **15 ml**
Soda to top up
Ice cubes

Method

Pour all the ingredients into a shaking glass with ice cubes. Shake well and pour into a glass.

Garnish Orange slice
Glass Frosted Pisa

Nutty Mango Smoothie

Ingredients

Yoghurt **100 ml**
Mango, fresh **60 gm**
Cashewnut **15 gm**
Cardamom powder **3 gm**

Method

Blend yoghurt, fresh mango, and cardamom powder. Pour into a glass.

Garnish Cashewnuts
Glass Pilsner

Chicane

Ingredients
Watermelon **100 gm**
Basil **6 leaves**
Cranberry juice **120 ml**
Homemade cranberry & vanilla sugar* **10 gm**

Method
Muddle watermelon with basil. Add cranberry juice and crushed ice. Shake well and dust with homemade cranberry and vanilla sugar.

Garnish Basil sprig
Glass Pilsner

* This is a homemade caster sugar mix of vanilla pod and dried cranberry.

Cardinal Punch

Ingredients

Cranberry juice **60 ml**
Orange juice **30 ml**
Lime juice **15 ml**
Ginger ale to top up

Method

Pour all the juices over ice in a glass and top up with ginger ale.

Garnish Orange and lemon slice
Glass Pilsner

Just Dew It Smoothie

Ingredients

Yoghurt **100 ml**
Orange **25 gm**
Musk melon **60 gm**
Honey dew **50 gm**

Method

Blend yoghurt, orange, and musk melon together. Pour into a glass.

Garnish Musk melon slice
Glass Pilsner

Berry Berry Smoothie

Ingredients

Yoghurt **100 ml**
Blueberry **25 gm**
Strawberry **50 gm**
Honey **50 ml**

Method

Blend yoghurt, blueberry and strawberry. Pour into a glass.

Garnish Mint sprig
Glass Pilsner

Virgin Devil

Ingredients

Grenadine syrup **10 ml**
Sugar syrup **10 ml**
Lemon juice **10 ml**
Ginger ale to top up
Crushed ice

Method

Add all the ingredients, one by one, into a glass over lots of ice.

Garnish Dry red chilli
Glass Highball

Tropical Cooler

Ingredients

Mint syrup **10 ml**
Pineapple juice **90 ml**
Lemonade **120 ml**
Ice cubes

Method

Put the ice in the glass, add mint syrup, pineapple juice, and top up with lemonade.

Garnish Pineapple slice
Glass Cocktail

Spiced Mocktails

Cinnamon Tea Punch

Ingredients

Apple juice **1 cup**
Apricot nectar **1 cup**
Cinnamon sticks **2**
Cinnamon flavoured herbal tea **2 cups**

Method

Combine apple juice, apricot nectar, and cinnamon sticks in a saucepan and simmer on low heat for 1-2 minutes, stirring occasionally. Add the tea and stir to mix all the ingredients. Remove the cinnamon sticks and pour the mixture in 4 glasses; sprinkle with ground cinnamon, if desired.

Garnish Cinnamon stick
Glass Brandy balloon

Chocolato

Ingredients

Black coffee **60 ml**
Chocolate syrup **20 ml**
Sugar syrup **20 ml**
Cinnamon powder **1 tsp**
Whipped cream **2 tbsp**

Method

Shake the coffee, chocolate syrup, sugar syrup, cinnamon powder with ice. Strain into a glass. Top up with whipped cream.

Garnish Chocolate shaves
Glass Old-fashioned

Honey Chilli Berry

Ingredients

Cranberry juice **120 ml**
Apple juice **120 ml**
Honey **15 ml**
Dried red chilies **3 pieces**

Method

Put all the ingredients in a Boston shaker with ice, shake well. Double strain into a tall glass half filled with crushed ice.

Garnish Apple slice
Glass Tall

Passion Delight

Ingredients

Passion fruit **1**
Chillies, chopped **2 tsp**
Lemon juice **5 ml**
Honey **a dash**
Ginger ale to top up
Ice cubes

Method

Add passion fruit and green chillies in a cocktail shaker. Add a dash of honey. Muddle all the ingredients together. Add a dash of lemon juice and pour into a glass filled with ice.

Garnish Chilli
Glass Tom Collins

Masala Watermelon Granita

Ingredients

Watermelon juice **180 ml**
Rock salt **1 tsp**
Lemon juice **5 ml**
Ice cubes

Method

Blend all the ingredients with ice and pour into a glass.

Garnish Watermelon slice coated with rock salt
Glass Old-fashioned

Grape Sparkle

Ingredients
Grape juice **120 ml**
Olives, green **5**
Lemon juice, fresh **5 ml**
Club soda to top up
Ice cubes

Method
Pour grape juice into a shaker. Add olives and muddle olives in the grape juice to extract the flavour. Fill a glass with lots of ice cubes. Pour the muddled ingredients into the glass and add lemon juice. Top up with club soda.

Garnish Olives
Glass Wine

Summer Belleni

Ingredients

Mint **5-10 leaves**
Cucumber, diced **2 tsp**
Lemon juice **5 ml**
Ginger ale to top up
Ice cubes

Method

Take cucumber and mint leaves in a cocktail shaker. Add lemon juice. Muddle all ingredients together with ice cubes. Pour into a table salt-rimmed glass. Top up with ginger ale.

Garnish Cucumber stick
Glass Tom Collins

Ginger-Cinnamon Lemonade

Ingredients

Ginger, juliennes **4-5**
Green cardamom powder **½ tsp**
Lemon juice **30 ml**
Sugar syrup **15 ml**
Soda to top up

Method

In a tall glass muddle ginger juliennes with green cardamom powder. Add lemon juice and sugar syrup. Top up with soda.

Garnish Ginger juliennes
Glass Highball

Beach Blast

Ingredients

Guava juice **90 ml**
Rock salt **1 gm**
Ginger juice **10 ml**
Ginger ale to top up

Method

Add lots of ice in a rock salt-rimmed glass. Pour the guava juice, fresh ginger juice, and a pinch of rock salt. Top up with ginger ale and serve.

Garnish Guava wedge
Glass Old-fashioned

Tamarind Shikanji

Ingredients
Tamarind extract **30 ml**
Chaat masala **2 tsp**
Lemon juice **10 ml**
Sugar syrup **10 ml**
Water **240 ml**
Ice cubes

Method
In a tall glass add all the ingredients with ice. Add water, stir and serve.

Garnish Tamarind pod
Glass Highball

Cool Buzz

Ingredients
Cucumber chunks **10 gm**
Basil, fresh **5-6 leaves**
Cloves **2**
Lemon juice **5 ml**
Sugar syrup **10 ml**
Tonic water to top up
Crushed ice

Method
In a tall glass muddle the cucumber, basil leaves, and cloves. Add crushed ice, lemon juice, sugar syrup and top up with tonic water.

Garnish Lemon slice
Glass Highball

Chaat Masala Punch

Ingredients

Lemon chunks **5 pieces**
Mint **5 sprigs**
Chaat masala **a pinch**
Black salt **a pinch**
Cucumber **2 slices**
Soda water **a splash**

Method

Muddle together lemon chunks and mint leaves. Add chaat masala, black salt, cucumber slices, and top up with soda. Stir well to mix all the ingredients.

Garnish Lemon slice and mint sprig
Glass Tom Collins

Delhi Pleasure

Ingredients
Pineapple juice **100 ml**
Khus syrup **5 ml**
Cream, fresh **5 ml**

Method
Blend pineapple juice with fresh cream and khus syrup.

Garnish Pineapple slice
Glass Highball

Classy Red Tea

Ingredients

Grape juice **1 quart**
Apple juice **1 quart**
Cinnamon stick **1 large**
Cloves **4**
Bergamot tea **½ tsp**

Method

In a pan cook grape juice, apple juice, cinnamon stick, and 4 cloves on low heat. Add bergamot tea and let it brew for 5-10 minutes. Strain and serve hot in mugs with orange slices.

Garnish Orange slice
Glass Mugs

Heart of Fire

Ingredients

Passion fruit **1**

Green chillies, chopped **2 tbsp**

Honey **a dash**

Lemon juice **5 ml**

Ginger ale to top up

Ice cubes

Method

Add passion fruit and green chillies into a cocktail shaker. Add the honey. Muddle all the ingredients together. Add lemon juice and pour into a glass filled with ice.

Garnish Green chilli

Glass Tom Collins

Black Magic

Ingredients
Orange juice **120 ml**
Black currant syrup **60 ml**
Cumin powder **a pinch**
Chaat masala **a pinch**
Black salt **a pinch**
Lemon juice **5 ml**
Soda water **a splash**
Ice cubes

Method
Shake all the ingredients together in shaker with ice. Pour into a glass and top up with soda.

Garnish Orange slice
Glass Tom Collins

Spiceale

Ingredients
Basil **8-10 leaves**
Ginger, juliennes **6-7**
Lemon juice **15 ml**
Sugar syrup **15 ml**
7up to top up
Ice cubes

Method
Muddle basil leaves and ginger juliennes. Add sugar syrup and lemon juice in a cooler glass. Add ice and top up with 7up.

Garnish Basil leaves and lemon slice
Glass Old-fashioned

Note Ginger refreshes the drink and adds a strong taste and aroma to it.

Sala Thai

Ingredients
Lemon grass **4**
Mint **6 leaves**
Lemon juice **15 ml**
Sugar syrup **15 ml**
Soda to top up
Ice cubes

Method
Muddle lemon grass and mint leaves, balance well with lemon juice and sugar syrup. Shake well with ice and strain into a glass filled with ice cubes. Top up with soda.

Garnish Lemon grass stick
Glass Tom Collins

Pine Khus Marriage

Ingredients
Pineapple chunks, fresh **4 pieces**
Khus syrup **30 ml**
Cumin powder and rock salt **a pinch each**
Ice cubes

Method
In a mixing jar, add all the ingredients along with ice and blend thoroughly, pour into a glass.

Garnish A mint sprig
Glass Royal highball

Spice Up Your Life

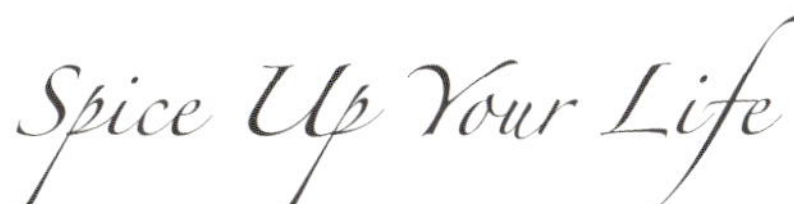

Ingredients

Green chillies, fresh, chopped **2**
Mint leaves, fresh **a few leaves**
Lemon, cut into chunks **1**
Mint syrup **15 ml**
Sprite to top up
Crushed ice

Method

Take a cocktail shaker and put the green chilies. Add mint leaves, lemon chunks, and mint syrup. Muddle all the ingredients in the shaker with a muddler. Add in crushed ice and shake well. Pour the mixture into a glass.

Garnish Lemon spiral
Glass Stemless Champagne Flute

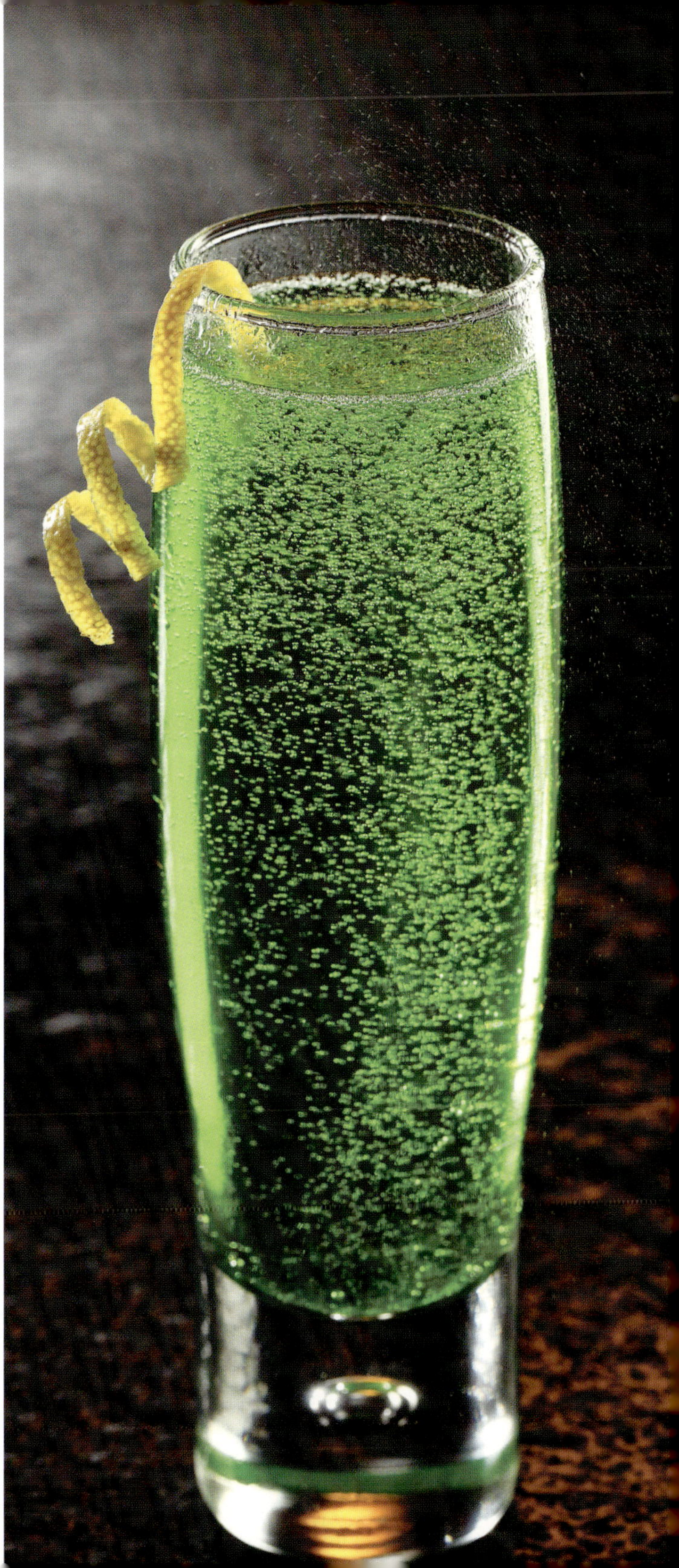

Guava Mary

Ingredients

Guava juice **100 ml**
Worcestershire sauce **a dash**
Tabasco sauce **a dash**
Lemon juice **5 ml**
Chaat masala **1 tsp**
Salt **¼ tsp**
Mint leaves for garnish
Crushed ice

Method

Blend all the ingredients and pour into a glass rimmed with chaat masala.

Garnish Mint sprig and chaat masala
Glass Rolly Polly

Guava Spice

Ingredients

Guava juice **100 ml**
Roasted cumin seeds **15 gm**
Black salt **5 gm**

Method

Grind roasted cumin seeds. Put ground cumin, black salt, and guava juice in a mixing glass. Shake well and pour the mixture in black salt-rimmed glass.

Garnish Guava slice
Glass Highball

Moksha Delight

Ingredients

Fresh sweet lime juice **160 ml**
Honey **20 ml**
Basil **5 leaves**
Ginger, juliennes **5**
Ginger juice, fresh **5 ml**
Crushed ice

Method

Put all the ingredients in a blender with 2 cupfuls of crushed ice and blend.

Garnish Sweet lime wedge
Glass Beer pilsner

Wasabi Mary in the Pool!

Ingredients

Canned tomato juice **90 ml**
Tabasco and
Worcestershire sauce **a few drops**
Wasabi sauce **a few drops**
Lemon juice **10 ml**
Black peppercorns,
freshly ground **a pinch**
Celery salt to rim the glass
Ice cubes

Method

Take a glass and rim it with celery salt and make four dots of Wasabi sauce on the rim. Add the ice cubes in the glass and pour the tomato juice. Add the lemon juice and stir it once. Then add the ground black pepper and drops of Wasabi sauce.

Garnish Celery stick and mint
Glass Tom Collins

Panna Punch

Ingredients
Mango panna **90 ml**
Roasted cumin **½ tsp**
Limca to top up
Crushed ice

Method
Pour Limca over the panna in a glass. Add the crushed ice and roasted cumin.

Garnish Raw mango slice
Glass Tall

Kylin Virgin Mary

Ingredients
Kaffir lime, chopped **1**
Celery stick, chopped (finger sized) **half**
Ginger, chopped **½ tsp**
Salt **a pinch**
Tabasco **3 dashes**
Worcestershire sauce **3 dashes**
Lemon juice **15 ml**
Ice cubes

Method
Pour all the ingredients over ice into a shaker, shake vigorously and strain.

Garnish Lemon wedge and celery stick
Glass Rock

Green Forest

Ingredients
Mint **10 leaves**
Khus syrup **20 ml**
Lemon juice **10 ml**
Sugar syrup **5 ml**
Green chillies **2 pieces**
Sprite **1 can**

Method
Take the mint leaves, khus syrup, lemon juice, and sugar syrup. Blend and pour into a glass. Float a chilli and top up with Sprite.

Garnish Chilli
Glass Tom Collins

Magical Ming

Ingredients
Guava juice **180 ml**
Pineapple juice **90 ml**
Black salt **a pinch**
Green chillies **2**
Ice cubes

Method
Pour all the ingredients over ice into a shaker, shake vigorously and strain into a glass with lots of ice.

Garnish Coriander leaves
Glass Tom Collins

Spicy Guava Breeze

Ingredients

Guava juice **200 ml**
Lemon juice **15 ml**
Worcestershire sauce **2 dashes**
Tabasco sauce **2 dashes**
Chaat masala **a pinch**
Ice cubes

Method

Take cubes of ice in a chaat masala rimmed rock glass, add Tabasco, Worcestershire sauce, lemon juice, and guava juice. Then add chaat masala. Stir and serve.

Garnish Mint sprig
Glass Old-fashioned

Hangover Drinks

Bold Eye

Ingredients

Coffee (use tonic water to make coffee) **20 ml**
Egg yolk **1**
Orange juice **30 ml**
Salt **to taste**
Lemon juice **10 ml**
Black peppercorns, freshly ground to taste
Crushed ice

Method

Shake all the ingredients together with crushed ice in the shaker and pour into a glass. Sprinkle a little pepper on top.

Garnish Freshly ground black pepper
Glass Highball
Tip Quinine present in the tonic water mixed with coffee helps reduce hangover instantly. This effect can be lessened by drinking plenty of water after this hangover drink.

Magical Ginger Ale

Ingredients

Watermelon chunks **1 bowl**
Pineapple chunks **1 bowl**
Lemon juice **30 ml**
Black pepper **1 tsp**
Rock salt **1 tsp**
Green coriander **1 sprig**
Ginger ale to top up
Ice cubes

Method

Blend all the ingredients well. Pour and serve.

Garnish Coriander leaves
Glass Tall
Note Pepper is a natural diuretic to cleanses your system, also increases the production of hydrochloric acid preventing heartburn and throwing up. A little fizz with ginger ale gets your eyes wide open.

Grateful Banana

Ingredients

Banana **1**
Green tea water **100 ml**
Ginger powder **1 tsp**
Sugar **1 tbsp**
Salt **1 tsp**
Lemon juice **30 ml**
Ice cubes

Method

Blend all the ingredients together to get a rich creamy drink. Pour into a tall glass. Gulp it or sip it.

Garnish Coriander Leaves
Glass Tall
Note Sugar and salt make a lethal combo of electrolytes which helps the body to re-hydrate fast. Ginger is a great tool for natural healing and boosting your immune system naturally.

Red Eye

Ingredients
Ice **4-5 cubes**
Lemon juice, fresh **15 ml**
Tabasco and Worcestershire sauce **a dash**
Celery salt **a pinch**
Tomato juice **100 ml**
Egg yolk **1**

Method
Mix all the ingredients together in a salt-rimmed glass. Stir well. Slowly slide in the egg yolk before serving.

Garnish Mint sprig
Glass Old-fashioned

Rainforest

Ingredients

Ginger **3 gm**
Pineapple **10-15 gm**
Coriander **½ tsp**
Celery sticks **4-5″**
Pineapple juice, fresh **100 ml**

Method

Blend all the ingredients together and pour into a glass.

Garnish Pineapple rings
Glass Tom collins

Bullshot

Ingredients

Beef consomme or chicken stock **60 ml**
Tabasco sauce **8 dashes**
Lemon juice, fresh **15 ml**
Worcestershire sauce **4 dashes**
Black pepper, freshly grated **12 time grinds of a peppermill**
Tomato juice to top up
Ice cubes

Method

Rim the glass with celery salt (regular salt if celery salt is not available) and fill up the glass with clean ice. Add the ingredients as mentioned above. Stir the drink gently and serve.

Garnish Celery stalk and Carrot stick
Glass Pilsner

Wake Me Up

Ingredients
Lemon juice, fresh **30 ml**
Salt **½ tsp**
Angostura bitter **3 drops**
Water **230 ml**

Method

Pour freshly squeezed lemon juice and salt into a glass. Add 3 drops of Angostura bitter. Finally add water to the mix and serve.

Garnish Lemon slice
Glass Tom collins

Bavarian Tomato

Ingredients
Tomato juice **90 ml**
Sauerkrat juice **90 ml**
Caraway seeds, ground **1 tsp**
Tabasco sauce **a few drops**
Celery stick **1**
Ice cubes

Method

Put all the ingredients together with ice cubes in the shaker, shake well and pour the drink in a salt-rimmed glass.

Garnish Celery stick
Glass Old-fashioned
Note Well seasoned pick me up drink to counteract a hangover.

Goodbye Hangover

Ingredients

Almonds, crushed **4-6**
Ginger, fresh, crushed **10 gm**
Lemon **2 pcs**
Mint **6-8 leaves**
Honey **20 ml**
Orange juice **150 ml**
Lemon wedges for garnish
Ice cubes

Method

Muddle almonds, ginger, lemon, and mint in a glass. Add ice and honey and top up with orange juice.

Garnish Lemon wedge
Glass Highball

Virgin Mojito

Ingredients

Lemon **4 wedges**
Mint **10 leaves**
Demerara sugar **2 tbsp**
Lemon juice **10 ml**
Soda to top up
Crushed ice

Method

Muddle lemon wedges, mint leaves, and demerara sugar. Fill the glass with crushed ice and add lemon juice. Top up with soda.

Garnish Lemon wedge and mint sprigs
Glass Rock

Down Under

Ingredients
Lemon juice **5 ml**
Angostura bitter **2 dashes**
Worcestershire sauce **2 dashes**
Tabasco **2 dashes**
Orange juice **15 ml**
Cranberry juice **15 ml**
Tonic water to top up
Ice cubes

Method
Pour all ingredients over ice cubes and top up with tonic water.

Garnish Orange slice
Glass Pilsner

Good Morning!

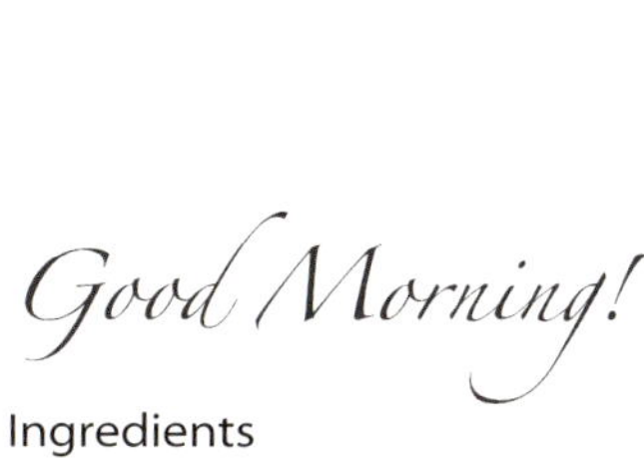

Ingredients

Carrot juice **200 ml**
Angostura bitter **5 drops**
Grenadine syrup **10 ml**
Cranberry juice **100 ml**
Egg yolk **1**

Method

Pour all the ingredients except egg yolk in a glass. Stir and before serving add the egg yolk.

Garnish Mint sprig
Glass Tom Collins
Variation Instead of carrot juice you can put tomato juice to alter the taste.

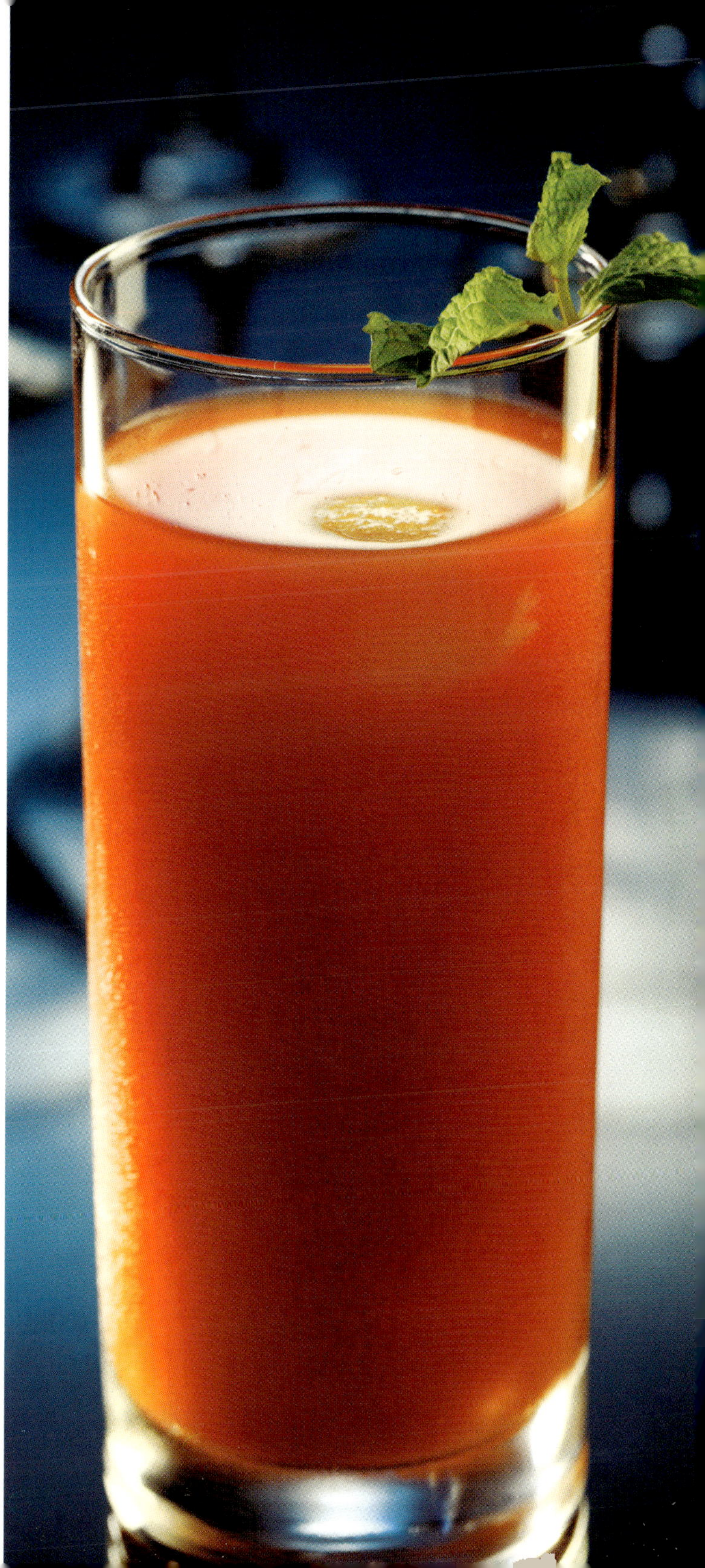

Mango Trick

Ingredients

Mango, ripe, peeled, cut, diced **½**
Carrot juice **60 ml**
Pineapple juice **60 ml**
Orange juice, fresh **60 ml**
Lemon juice, fresh **20 ml**
Still mineral water
Ice cubes

Method

Put mango pieces in a blender, add all other ingredients except water, a scoop of ice-cubes and blend. Using the lid to stop the ice tumbling into a glass, pour the mixture into a glass filled with fresh ice. Pour till ¾th full. Add the water to dilute the mixture a little. Stir and serve.

Garnish Cherry
Glass Goblet

Mr Aura Hangover Fight

Ingredients

Tomato juice **1 large can**
Vinegar **3 tbsp**
Juice of lemon **1**
Onion **4 slices**
Sugar **3 tbsp**
Celery stalks, chopped into small pieces **4**
Tabasco sauce **2 tsp**
Salt and pepper **to taste**

Method

Mix all of the ingredients in a container and let it stand overnight in the refrigerator. Strain and serve in a glass.

Garnish Celery Stalk
Glass Cocktail

To & Fro

Ingredients
Coriander **3 sprigs**
Lemon **3-4 wedges**
Rock salt **a pinch**
Passion fruit purée **60 ml**
Orange juice, fresh **90 ml**
Crushed ice

Method
Muddle coriander with lemon wedges and a pinch of rock salt in a tall glass. Add crushed ice half-way up the glass and pour passion fruit purée and orange juice, stirring continuously. Garnish and serve.

Garnish Orange rind, coriander sprig, and passion fruit seeds.
Glass Tom Collins

Grape Fruit Lemonade

Ingredients

Grape fruit juice **120 ml**
Angostura bitter **a dash**
Lemon juice **15 ml**
Sugar syrup **15 ml**
Soda to top up
Ice cubes

Method

Shake all the ingredients except soda with ice in a cocktail shaker and pour into a glass with ice. Top up with soda.

Garnish Grape fruit slice
Glass Tom collins
Tip Little salt in the drink might be satisfying to keep the bitterness of grape fruit juice intact.

Mixed Apples and Celery Detoxifier

Ingredients

Green apple **1**

Red apple **1**

Celery stalk **1**

Method

In a juicer process a green and red apple with a celery stalk to extract the juices. Strain in a chilled glass and squeeze half a lemon.

Garnish Apple slices

Glass Cocktail

Note Enjoy this drink to get rid of a hangover. It also helps in fighting headaches and stomach upsets. It is a perfect energy booster. Try it after workouts.

Photograph: Roy Raymond Hende

A Word of Thanks

This book would not have been possible but for the secret recipes shared very generously by the bartenders of:

Café Delhi Heights, New Delhi, NCR
Caperberry Restaurant & Tapas Lounge, Bengaluru
Clarion Collection, New Delhi
Courtyard by Marriott, Chennai
Courtyard by Marriott, Hyderabad
Courtyard by Marriott, Gurgaon
Crowne Plaza New Delhi Rohini
Crowne Plaza Today Gurgaon
Crowne Plaza Today, New Delhi
Ellipsis Mumbai
Eros managed by Hilton New Delhi Nehru Place
Fairmont Jaipur
Fava Restaurant, Bengaluru
Goa Marriott Resort & Spa
Grand Hyatt Goa
Hakkasan Mumbai
Hilton Garden Inn New Delhi/Saket
Hyatt Regency, New Delhi
Hyatt Regency, Chennai
Hyatt Regency, Mumbai
Hyderabad Marriott Hotel & Convention Centre
Ignis Restaurant & Bar, New Delhi
ITC Gardenia, Bengaluru
ITC Sonar, Kolkata
ITC Mughal, Agra
Jaipur Marriott
Jolly Rogers Lounge & Bar, Gurgaon
JW Marriott Chandigarh
JW Marriott Hotel, Mumbai
Kingdom of Dreams, Gurgaon
Kylin Restaurant, New Delhi
Le Méridien Jaipur
Le Méridien New Delhi
Lodi—The Garden Restaurant, New Delhi
Mocha Arthouse, New Delhi
Move & Pick Hotel Bangalore
Olive Bar & Kitchen, Mumbai
Olive Bar & Kitchen, New Delhi
Olive Beach, Bengaluru
Park Hyatt Goa Resort & Spa
Park Plaza, Noida
Pullman Gurgaon Central Park
Radisson Blu Hotel, New Delhi Paschim Vihar
Radisson Blu Hotel, Noida
Rainforest Resto-Bar, Mumbai
Renaissance Mumbai
Renaissance Mumbai Convention Centre Hotel
Set'z Restaurant & Bar, New Delhi
Sheraton Bangalore Hotel At Brigade Gateway
Shiro Restaurant, New Delhi
Smoke House Grill, New Delhi
Sofitel Mumbai BKC
Spot Lounge, Kitchen & Bar, Gurgaon
Swissôtel Kolkata
Taj Palace Hotel, New Delhi
Taj Rambagh Palace, Jaipur
The Claridges, New Delhi
The Claridges, Surajkund, Delhi, NCR
The Grand, New Delhi
The Imperial—New Delhi
The Lalit, New Delhi
The Lalit, Mumbai
The Leela Palace, Mumbai
The Leela Palace, New Delhi
The Oberoi, Bengaluru
The Park, Bengaluru
The Park, Chennai
The Suryaa, New Delhi
The Westin Mumbai Garden City
The Metropolitan Hotel & Spa, New Delhi
The Westin Mumbai Garden City
The Westin Pune Koregaon Park
Trident Mumbai
Valhalla Restaurant Lounge, Mumbai
Vinoteca by Sula, Mumbai
Vivanta by Taj—Ambassador, New Delhi
Vivanta by Taj—President, Mumbai

INDEX

If you have always stood stupefied, wondering at the skill of the 'magician' behind the bar counter as he has gone about creating the perfect concoction of taste and colour; with a cup of this and a dash of that, then *Cheers! 365 Cocktails and Mocktails* gives you the opportunity to create your own magic to liven up an occasion. Guiding you on exactly what and how much to mix, this book also takes a step forward to explain the kind of glasses that should be used when serving these 'creations.' With inputs from the most talented bartenders across the country, who strongly believe that 'Drinking is an art and requires practice to know how to drink, what to drink and when to drink,' this book lets you join their elusive club to mix the most visually stunning drinks! A complete page turner, this collection promises to truly knock you off your feet!

Sharmila Chand is a Delhi based freelance journalist who hotfoots across the world to satiate her interest in almost everything on this earth - Travel, Art & Culture, Music, Spa and of course, Food, Food and more Food.

She loves to chat with chefs and bartenders and if they are good looking and cool dudes, she loses her heart too often! Know more about the author: www.sharmilachand.com